Education for Student Development

Jane Fried, *Editor*

NEW DIRECTIONS FOR STUDENT SERVICES
URSULA DELWORTH and GARY HANSON, *Editors-in-Chief*
Number 15, September 1981

Paperback sourcebooks in
The Jossey-Bass Higher Education Series

Jossey-Bass Inc., Publishers
San Francisco • Washington • London

Education for Student Development
Number 15, September 1981
    Jane Fried, *Editor*

New Directions for Student Services Series
Ursula Delworth and Gary R. Hanson, *Editors-in-Chief*

Copyright © 1981 by Jossey-Bass Inc., Publishers
             and
             Jossey-Bass Limited

Copyright under International, Pan American, and Universal
Copyright Conventions. All rights reserved. No part of
this issue may be reproduced in any form—except for brief
quotation (not to exceed 500 words) in a review or professional
work—without permission in writing from the publishers.

New Directions for Student Services (publication number USPS
449-070) is published quarterly by Jossey-Bass Inc., Publishers.
Second-class postage rates paid at San Francisco, California,
and at additional mailing offices.

Correspondence:
Subscriptions, single-issue orders, change of address notices,
undelivered copies, and other correspondence should be sent to
New Directions Subscriptions, Jossey-Bass Inc., Publishers,
433 California Street, San Francisco, California 94104.

Editorial correspondence should be sent to the Editors-in-Chief,
Ursula Delworth, University Counseling Service, Iowa
Memorial Union, University of Iowa, Iowa City, Iowa 52242
or Gary R. Hanson, Office of the Dean of Students,
Student Services Building, Room 101, University of Texas
at Austin, Austin, Texas 78712.

Library of Congress Catalogue Card Number LC 80-84302
International Standard Serial Number ISSN 0164-7970
International Standard Book Number ISBN 87589-863-7

Cover art by Willi Baum
Manufactured in the United States of America

Ordering Information

The paperback sourcebooks listed below are published quarterly and can be ordered either by subscription or single-copy.

Subscriptions cost $30.00 per year for institutions, agencies, and libraries. Individuals can subscribe at the special rate of $18.00 per year *if payment is by personal check.* (Note that the full rate of $30.00 applies if payment is by institutional check, even if the subscription is designated for an individual.) Standing orders are accepted.

Single copies are available at $6.95 when payment accompanies order, and *all single-copy orders under $25.00 must include payment.* (California, Washington, D.C., New Jersey, and New York residents please include appropriate sales tax.) For billed orders, cost per copy is $6.95 plus postage and handling. (Prices subject to change without notice.)

To ensure correct and prompt delivery, all orders must give either the *name of an individual* or an *official purchase order number.* Please submit your order as follows:

Subscriptions: specify series and subscription year.
Single Copies: specify sourcebook code and issue number (such as, IR8).

Mail orders for United States and Possessions, Latin America, Canada, Japan, Australia, and New Zealand to:
    Jossey-Bass Inc., Publishers
    433 California Street
    San Francisco, California 94104

Mail orders for all other parts of the world to:
    Jossey-Bass Limited
    28 Banner Street
    London EC1Y 8QE

New Directions for Student Services Series
Ursula Delworth and Gary R. Hanson, *Editors-in-Chief*

SS1 *Evaluating Program Effectiveness,* Gary R. Hanson
SS2 *Training Competent Staff,* Ursula Delworth
SS3 *Reducing the Dropout Rate,* Lee Noel
SS4 *Applying New Developmental Findings,* Lee Knefelkamp, Carole Widick, Clyde A. Parker
SS5 *Consulting on Campus,* M. Kathryn Hamilton, Charles J. Meade
SS6 *Utilizing Futures Research,* Frederick R. Brodzinski
SS7 *Establishing Effective Programs,* Margaret J. Barr, Lou Ann Keating
SS8 *Redesigning Campus Environments,* Lois Huebner
SS9 *Applying Management Techniques,* Cecelia H. Foxley
SS10 *Serving Handicapped Students,* Hazel Z. Sprandel, Marlin R. Schmidt
SS11 *Providing Student Services for the Adult Learner,* Arthur Shriberg

SS12 *Responding to Changes in Financial Aid Programs,* Shirley F. Binder
SS13 *Increasing the Educational Role of Residence Halls,* Gregory S. Blimling, John H. Schuh
SS14 *Facilitating Students' Career Development,* Vincent A. Harren, M. Harry Daniels, Jacqueline N. Buck

Contents

Developmental Instruction

Editor's Notes vii
Jane Fried

Chapter 1. Images of Learning 1
Roy P. Fairfield

New images of learning and new ways to focus on the process of understanding ourselves and the world constitute an uprooting of old ideas about what ought to happen in college classrooms.

Chapter 2. Principles of Design 11
Jane Fried

The design of developmental courses must be focused primarily on the developmental concerns of students and the teaching methods of faculty.

Chapter 3. Instructional Consultation 27
Deborah Simpson

Student development theory can provide a guide for helping faculty members understand how their students learn and how to tailor teaching methods to student learning styles.

Chapter 4. The Learning Dialogue: Teaching 39
Clyde A. Parker, Jeffrey M. Kreps

Students and teachers replace the "double monologue" with the dialogue about issues meaningful to both.

Chapter 5. The Learning Dialogue: Mentoring 49
Virginia Lester, Cynthia Johnson

Mentoring provides a model for a wholistic relationship between the student and the faculty member who can guide the student toward setting educational, life, and career goals.

Chapter 6. The Learning Dialogue: Evaluation 57
Timothy Taylor-Gaunder

Evaluation is a manageable task for developmental educators. There are even some useful "homemade" evaluation tools that can be used to supplement commercial instruments.

Chapter 7. Project Synergy 65
J. Eugene Knott, Douglas Daher

The University of Rhode Island conducts a program that helps freshmen develop college survival skills, improved interpersonal skills, and increased self-confidence.

Chapter 8. Self-Science Education 73
Gerald Weinstein

"Education of the Self" is a course that gives students the structure, skills, and emotional support to become self-scientists, observe their own behavior, experiment with new ways to behave, and evaluate the results.

Chapter 9. The Individual in Society: The Interdisciplinary 79
Studies Program
Norma Watkins

The I-Division program offers an interdisciplinary, experiential approach to helping community college students understand the self, the immediate community, and the larger society.

Chapter 10. Facts, Feelings, and Academic Credit 87
Margaret Barr, Jane Fried

Academic faculty and student-affairs administrators occupy different professional worlds; there are some methods for improving mutual understanding and communication between the two groups.

Chapter 11. Conclusions and Annotated References 103
Jane Fried

Index 109

Editor's Notes

Developmental Instruction is a phrase that has been used by many educational professions, yet remains filled with ambiguity and often signifies confusion. The phrase can indicate a range of activities from remediation in physical, mathematical, and verbal skills to instruction in interpersonal skills. The process of helping students to improve their level of cognitive complexity has also been included in developmental instruction (Widick, Knefelkamp, and Parker, 1975). For this volume, the broadest definition of developmental instruction has been chosen, one that aligns developmental education with humanistic education as described by the ancient Greeks: "Man[sic] is the measure of all things . . . If learning is placed in that context, man is free to evolve values, social systems, and philosophies of human nature which fit his needs, not those of the gods or oracles" (Fairfield, 1971, p. 5). All education that places the human being at the heart of the learning process, which asks questions about meaning, value, and the implications of knowledge, is, by definition, humanistic education. All teaching methods that contribute to the examination of meanings, values, and implications, and that subscribe to the notion that the inquiry *process* is more significant than finding the "right" answer, or product, are developmental methods.

Who engages in developmental instruction? (1) Student-affairs staff, counselors, and others who teach experiential courses that focus on aspects of the human condition; (2) faculty members in traditional academic disciplines who encourage students to apply what they have learned in class to significant problems in their lives and the life of their community; (3) teaching-improvement consultants who collaborate with faculty members to help them understand various levels of cognitive development and various types of learning styles.

Ideally, all members of the educational staff of a college or university can engage in developmental instruction if they are consciously attempting to help students grow in their understanding of themselves and the world around them, or helping them improve in their ability to think about those areas. In reality, much developmental instruction is conducted by members of the student-affairs staffs who are taking the training methods of human relations into the college classroom, or who are expanding the training programs with philosophy, psychology, literature, and any other dimension of human knowledge that seems relevant.

Special thanks to Lori Bartolucci and Eileen Wight for their outstanding secretarial services.

Developmental instruction is an art in the process of becoming more scientific. Methods for measuring development—ethical, cognitive, moral, emotional, interpersonal—are becoming more sophisticated and accurate. Measurement techniques need not be heavily dependent on the personality of the tester in order to yield satisfactory results. Teaching, however, has always been an art. Good teaching is dependent not only on the teacher's knowledge of subject matter but also on the teacher's ability to present information, evoke questions, provoke insight, and, in the case of life-skill education, to model behavior. The format of this volume reflects the synthesis of art and science necessary for developmental instruction.

New images of teaching and learning are basic to effective developmental instruction. Students and teachers must focus on the learning *process* rather than on knowledge as a *product* and get beyond their own training in the "mug-jug" theory of education. Roy Fairfield has strewn new images of teaching and learning in his chapter, reaching from the Golden Age of Greece to future learning networks (when colleges will occupy more time than space and education will be a life-long process). Fairfield challenges the reader to examine environmental imagery and self-imagery, academic slavery and computer liberation. He offers unusual images of the learning process as he encourages readers to chart a new course for college communities in which members learn from each other.

The chapters on design of developmental courses and instructional consultation are "how to" chapters. Fried presents a systematic approach to the process of creating and implementing developmental courses in academic environments. She guides the reader through the initial stages of conception, including ideas for curriculum development, feasibility testing, and methods for designing appropriate teaching/learning strategies. The chapter also includes applications of evaluation techniques to student performance and course effectiveness. Simpson presents another side of developmental instruction—consultation with faculty in the more traditional disciplines. She describes the Teaching Improvement Consultation Project (TIC) at the University of Minnesota, which provides a service to faculty by helping them to improve their teaching effectiveness and help their students improve their learning effectiveness. In the professional partnership, faculty are the content experts and educators in student development are the process experts. The TIC project helps to improve both the quality of academic life and the quality of professional relationships between student-affairs staff and faculty.

Images of mutual involvement between teachers, trainers, and students are present throughout this volume. Learning is seen as an active process that involves discussion, debate, and challenge. Clyde Parker and Jeffrey Kreps present one view of the learning dialogue that focuses on the interaction between student and teacher, not on the transmission of content. They assert that a major responsibility of faculty is to understand a student's point of view and attitude toward learning in order to find the most effective way to communicate with that student. The same piece of information can be communicated in many ways. The faculty member must know not only what to teach but also how to teach it to students whose learning and thinking styles vary widely.

Virginia Lester and Cynthia Johnson describe the learning dialogue from another point of view—the mentoring relationship. People who are involved in postsecondary education learn from each other in and out of class. They focus on academic information, career information, learning skills, and life skills. Students learn what to learn and how to learn from their mentors. They also gain some insight into the ways that another person uses to integrate living, working, learning, and planning for the future. The mentoring relationship in the college community can provide a guide for student-development education in many contexts. It provides a wholistic model for integrating living and learning.

Timothy Taylor-Gaunder extends the notion of the dialogue into the area of evaluation. Evaluation becomes a part of the planning process of a course, a manageable tool that instructors can use to help improve teaching methods. At several phases in planning and implementation of a course, the instructor gathers reactions from students and other members of the campus community about course effectiveness. The instructor and students can use this information to modify teaching methods and learning strategies as necessary. Many of the tools can be designed by the participants for maximum utility and minimum cost.

No *New Directions* volume is complete without chapters that describe realistic examples of programs illustrating the guidelines presented. This volume contains descriptions of three different developmental courses, two at universities and one at a community college. All the courses present clear methods for integrating knowledge about the outside world with self-knowledge, values, attitudes, and beliefs.

"Project Synergy," described by Doug Daher and Gene Knott, is a program designed to help freshmen at the University of Rhode Island develop college survival skills, improved interpersonal skills, and a clearer sense of themselves as emerging adults. The course focuses on increased responsibility for the self in such areas as time management, environmental awareness, physical health, and study skills. Students also examine developmental theory and study issues related to interpersonal intimacy, managing stress, life and career planning, and dealing with personal loss.

"Education of the Self," presented by Gerald Weinstein, is taught at the University of Massachusetts. This course focuses on helping students learn to observe their own behavior and assess its effectiveness in their efforts to achieve their own life goals. Students learn how to generate alternatives to current behavior, to develop a support system as they attempt to change, and to evaluate new behavior in terms of the same criteria for effectiveness.

The "Interdisciplinary Studies Program" ("I Division") at Miami-Dade Community College has a slightly different focus. Norma Watkins chaired a team of faculty members who designed an interdisciplinary course that helped students meet several of their general education requirements in one course: English, Social Science, Interdisciplinary Science (Physical and Biological), Human Relations, and Social Problems. The course was experientially based, integrated around life problems, and designed to help students apply what they were learning to significant life issues. The course is no longer in existence.

The final chapter by Barr and Fried is a "how to" chapter on a broader scale. Ideas and proposals for developmental instruction will have little or no impact on a college campus if their proponents are not wise in the ways of academic decision making and methods for achieving power and influence in the academic arena.

A word about nomenclature is necessary. Since people who provide out-of-class services to students are known by so many professional titles, student affairs personnel, student services personnel, and student personnel are considered interchangeable labels in this volume. Student-development education is considered "any experience in a learning environment which contributes to individual, group, or community growth and development in which a teacher and a student interact and which can be evaluated" (Crookston, 1970, p. 4). Any person who is employed by a postsecondary educational institution to participate in this type of education is a student-development educator when engaged in the processes so described. According to Crookston, student-development education should be "the central teaching function in the college . . . whether it produces credit or not; hence, the teacher of student development teaches in multiple situations, including the classroom" (1970, p. 7). The purpose of this volume is to shed new light on the many approaches to developmental instruction, that portion of student-development education which occurs as part of the accredited teaching/learning processes in higher education.

Jane Fried
Editor

References

Crookston, B. "An Organizational Model for Student Development." Paper presented at the Fall Conference of the Northwest College Personnel Association, Gearhart, Oregon, October 18, 1970.

Fairfield, R. (Ed.). *Humanistic Frontiers in American Education.* Englewood Cliffs, N.J.: Prentice-Hall, 1971.

Widick, C., Knefelkamp, L., and Parker, C. "The Counselor as Developmental Instructor." *Counselor Education and Supervision*, 1975, *14* (4), 286-296.

Jane Fried is the coordinator of student development, staff training, and research for the Office of Residential Life at the University of Connecticut. She is also an adjunct faculty member of the School of Education. She finished her doctoral coursework at the University of Connecticut under the advisorship of Burns Crookston. After his death, she completed her Ph.D. in counseling psychology through the Union Graduate School. She is the former chairperson of the New Professionals Task Force of the American College Personnel Association and the coordinator of the Burns Crookston Memorial Resource Collection at the University of Connecticut.

Static images of teaching and learning restrict creativity. Developmental instruction requires new images of education and a soaring vision of human potential.

Images of Learning

Roy P. Fairfield

"Lecturing professors are our modern gods and we offer them, just as the Aztecs did, the living bodies of our young" (West, 1980, p. 149).

Scene: An assistant dean of students enters a well-ordered classroom with seats neatly arranged in rows, says hello to a couple of students in the front row, climbs to the platform, opens his notes on the lectern, and begins lecturing about theories of group dynamics.

Scene: A resident counselor and an activities advisor move quickly about a huge and impersonal dormitory lounge, pulling and tugging sofas and stuffed chairs into a new configuration. Aware of the importance of space relationships, they are arranging structures much as a choreographer plans a ballet. About to conduct a course in group dynamics, they wish to illustrate their beliefs about the uses and abuses of space.

These two scenes illustrate radically different approaches to teaching and learning. The contrast between them illuminates two different sets of images about what ought to happen when teachers and students come together in a university. The descriptive language evokes a whole series of images (memories, textures, spaces, smells, and sounds) in which college graduates or university staff can immerse themselves. The language evokes the memory and the mental picture. In the same fashion, the language that we use to describe current experience shapes that experience, and the images we hold about a "college education" shape the way we go about our professional work on college campuses. Is "teaching" different from "helping someone learn"? Does a lecturer help people to learn in the same way a facilitator does?

Old, static images of learning and teaching tie us down and limit our creativity as we begin to create developmental courses for college students. Our own undergraduate images of teaching may easily anchor us in the past and prevent us from moving in another educational orbit. The next few pages are filled with images designed to provoke new ideas about learning and expanding awarenesses of multidimensional insight and growth. This chapter has two targets, the reader's sense of logic and the reader's sense of intuition/humor/curiosity/awe/irony/paradox. Both targets are one, the reader's consciousness. And the target is moving all the time.

Environmental Images and Self-Images

Every day we are immersed in images that elude our awareness until some external force focuses our attention on them. We use metaphors unthinkingly: wastelands of fatigue, political overkill, media saturation, white music, the crowded freeway as one long parking lot, the jammed subways as sardine cans, and on and on. Such images convey a depth of meaning that is greater than their literal significance. They increase the complexity of our consciousness. These "pictures in the mind," (Lippmann, 1955) can enlighten or deceive. For example, schools can be seen as learning arenas. (Does the image of the arena suggest a place where Christians compete against lions, or athletes against each other?) Over the centuries school images have become value-laden. At the elementary level, the little red schoolhouse has mellowed into positive, multifaceted learning (from teachers and peers). High schools have gradually metamorphosed from simple, closed spaces of one or two stories into sprawling, ranchlike structures, with communication "pods" (pseudopods?), media terminals, and every other manner of teaching machine. In higher education, ivy walls and ivory towers evoke tradition, while textbooks and lecture notes connote foundation stones. Both the library and the faculty contain knowledge that is converted into coins of the realm—academic credit. We pay homage to the Cartesian split of mind and body, which separates living from learning despite evidence that the effort is futile. And decade after decade, critics, especially from the student-service side of the campus, insist that we need to extend the learning context beyond the classroom walls and the lecture system. Was Woodrow Wilson correct when he defined the lecture as the means by which the professor's notes reach the students' notebooks without going through the mind of either? Was Stephen Leacock's observation accurate that a college education was what you have left over after you have forgotten all you knew? Indeed, it is tempting to laugh much of traditional teaching out of existence, yet it is more constructive to evolve a whole new cornucopia of images as valuable searchlights for expanding and sharpening awareness and insight. This process should enable student services educators to become more aware of their own contributions to student development and education whenever they find themselves in a classroom or other teaching environment. New images of teaching and learning, content and process, should also encourage student-development educators to throw off their own "educational baggage" and grow beyond the methods that their professors used on them.

Scene: A resident counselor, remembering a brilliant psychology professor whom she admired, attempted to emulate him. She worked twenty hours to develop a lecture that would be the climax to her counseling course. *Result:* To her it "went over like the proverbial lead balloon." *Result:* flight. *Result:* She needed more counseling than her students. *Moral:* The method must match the subject. The process should be as exciting as the content.

Academic Slavery and Computer Liberation

Classroom teachers and other merchants of learning may have created academic slavery, even as they fought for academic freedom. Student services educators are not immune to rigid mind sets. In teaching developmental courses, be wary of the academic slavery of your own mind locked into your undergraduate memory. It is not too far-fetched to describe many a classroom as four bare walls and a lecture—with the assumption that something important is happening. It is time for the image of dialogue to replace the image of many lectures. Students, staff, and faculty can respond to new information together, with each leading the way at different times. The explosion of electronic data-gathering devices and data-classification systems has liberated students and teachers alike from the slavery to lecture and text. We have long known that selective perception makes the value of the lecture highly questionable. We have long known that so much knowledge is available to everybody, that the professor-as-perambulating-encyclopedia or the dean-as-mastermind are anachronistic images. We know, too, that the incredible power of the computer and the speed by which it is being adopted in every type of field casts even further shadows on another fundamental assumption: that university personnel know best what students should learn and how they should behave.

The electronic revolution, of course, raises many specters. In today's world it is foolish to ignore or oppose computer imagery such as "input" or "printout," and electronic imagery such as "feedback," words whose magic in proper mouths will impress the technicians and frighten others. Computers, after all, can be the servants of all humans since they can store information and regurgitate it much more rapidly than human brains can comprehend. But the imagery and the machines must be employed for humans, not against them. Their value is to extend self-awareness of our own potential, the linking of facts to theories, of lectures to the world, of learners on both sides of the classroom desk or chair.

We need to expand learning imagery in both qualitative and quantitative dimensions. Our new images must include feelings as well as facts, process as well as content, organisms as well as mechanisms. A sense of the changes can be evoked by imagining:

- Rivers as well as ponds.
- Seas as well as bogs.
- Waving wheat fields as well as calm meadows.
- Kinesthetics as well as statics.
- Calculus and exponential relationships as well as arithmetic.
- Impression and sensation as well as conception.
- Dynamic daring and risking as well as cool security.
- Enthusiasm and hot sweats as well as cold logic.
- Manifestos evolving as well as credos controlling.
- Networks expanding and contrasting as well as circles confining (Fairfield, 1976, p. 210).

On numerous levels of experience and imagination, we must learn to develop a rhythm that allows motion as well as rest and denies the probability of academic slavery.

We have started to do this. The image "university without walls" begins to frame an arena in which learning can take place; the arena can be anywhere in space/time/consciousness. By using the term *facilitator* to describe both classroom and nonclassroom teachers who do, indeed, connect learners with optimal learning situations, we have acknowledged the creating of awareness of those who learn together, from the environment and each other. The specialist-as-resource suggests that learners must extend their own efforts if they are to gain knowledge, skill, and understanding. Learning has become an extension of the learner as well as an extension of facilitative energy.

Some institutions and professors are now beginning to recognize "life experience" and are hence credentialing it. External-degree and elderhostel programs, emeritus universities, and neighborhood learning centers all suggest that learning is a life-long program in living and examining life. So, we have begun! And we may wish to notice the flowing character of images such as continuing, facilitating, life-longing—images consistent with process notions, rivers, brooks, seas, kinesthetics, enthusiasms, networking, seeing, smelling, thinking. Persons approaching retirement might well change their own mind sets as they participate in these life-long learning activities. By abandoning normal images of static health, static life, and static sitting on a shelf, we can make "re-FIRE-ment" a time for refiring energy furnaces, a time for reinventing the second half of life, a time for setting new learning goals that advance with each new achieving. In developmental education, all learners can stay flexible, excited, involved, and fresh, if not chronologically young.

Learning from and with Each Other

Any professor and any student, learning virtually the same skills and knowledge concurrently (though in different contexts), may well be perceived by selves and others as co-learners who are sharing power and not rationing it. But even that does not go far enough. Each human in a learning context needs to be aware of personal readiness for making connections to one's own life history, to life histories of others, and to wisdom about the human condition. The power of this metaphor lies in its many meanings, whose connections may be as tenuous as the half hitch in a weaving or the droplet of water in a river moving toward the sea. Hence, here is an expansion of some ideas about learning together.

Learning Moments. Every waking and sleeping moment, in or out of a classroom or university, is a potential learning moment if we will but focus upon the how to make it such. The "how" must transcend mere gimmickry and move to fundamental questions of existence. Hence, it is a matter of learning that extends beyond increasing efficiency when adding three and three to recognizing intensely how one's mind and body make one a vital creature in space and time and psyche. Even the unconscious terrain can be explored through dream records and Jungian insight. Vitality flows from our sleeping levels of consciousness, allowing us to be aware of gold mines and goal mines in our psychic rivers.

Static Residency. Classical images of "residency" are static and no longer have as much utility as they once did. Such images connote and denote spaces such as residence halls, fraternities and sororities, campuses, counseling centers, classrooms, and libraries. A bachelor's degree can be acquired by remaining in a college or university long enough to accumulate 124 semester hours of campus occupation and accretion. Such imagery and the resulting confinement is too restricting. Such concepts as "course," "credit hours," "credentialing criteria," "contact hours," and "internship year" need exploding, for they are frequently so Procrustean that they cramp the human psyche. However valuable they may have been, they no longer obtain in a world where the halflife of knowledge diminishes by quantum leaps, especially in the practical arts, the natural and social sciences. The disjuncture between the process and content approaches to learning may be painful.

Scene: The teaching assistant in a freshman communication course, given an opportunity to "teach" a class while his professor was at a convention reading a paper, chose to break the class of sixty-two into four groups, each group being asked to evolve a critique of the knowledge acquired thus far, and then to choose a spokesperson to "report" to the whole class at the end of the ninety-minute period. *Result:* a devastating attack on the absent professor and a long bill of particulars with documentary support. *Result:* a furious professor who threatened to take the assistantship away from the graduate student, even though the student reminded the professor that they had agreed to this topic before he left. *Result:* more punitive action on the part of the professor—more quizzes, exams, no further discussion groups. *Result:* a devastated T.A. who was not quite so sure he wanted to become a student-development worker and collect "all that pain."

Charting a Course. Process is product and the product may be the learning process! Traditional professors and those who emulate them sometimes focus so heavily upon "bodies of knowledge" that they forget they are living manifestations of the Heisenberg notion; they are part of the problem as well as the solution. Their attitudes toward their own learning and lecturing and counseling techniques frequently distort the very stuff of learning. Developmental instructors can never forget one fundamental principle of McLuhan, "The medium is [at least part of] the message" (1967). It sometimes comes down to the art and science of arranging the scripts, much as an orchestra conductor does. Since we spend all too much of our lives doing what somebody else decides is "good for us," we need to become our own cartographers and navigators, never forgetting that we cannot invent latitude, longitude, or the North Star, but that we can use those concepts to plot our own constellations of learning skills, knowledge, and goals. If we must refer to maps and charts that previous generations have evolved, we will. But what are the risks of letting others set our learning compasses? Why not do it jointly by determining criteria collaboratively? If we must fall back upon competency-based concepts, what does it mean to develop competency-based self-education? If the language of movement and mapping does not suffice, how will the legal language of learning contracts serve?

Learning from Experience. Learners gain confidence and a greater sense of self-worth if they perceive their experiences, and their very lives, as unique and significant. Hence, the author's own confidence and successful experience with himself and many students using dream-logging, day and night dreams, to touch the unconscious. We have used letter-writing to evolve writing competence, fantasy and metaphor to float one into poetry, picture taking or picture-painting, carpentry, needlework—in fact, *any* form of craftsmanship or artistry to catch the moods of earth and sky and weave our minds around them. John Dewey reminded us (1916) that something new *is* born in the universe if we reinvent the wheel, so long as we distinguish what that event does for us as individuals from its nature as social invention.

Learning to Heal. Symbolizing and imaging as well as craftsmanship and artistry are incredibly valuable, self-healing processes. For example, playing with words, punning, standing concepts on their heads, bending over to look between your legs to see the world behind you (Thoreau's prescription to cure worldly jaundice)—all are fun and constructive IF not directed against others. While many educators and psychologists may prefer to practice the "fallacy of misplaced concretion" (Whitehead, 1925) by putting learning and therapy into separate compartments, persons such as Carl and Stephanie Simonton (1978) working with cancer-ridden patients and Norman Cousins (1979) working on himself with humor conclude that health is a function of what we learn, how we learn it, and how we practice values that result from such learning. This, of course, raises many fundamental ethical questions for developmental teachers and students: What is *healthy* learning and living? What is the price of separating one's own field of knowledge from others in the name of status, power, or wealth? What are the social and ethical prices of looking with disdain upon the innovator (such as Marx or Einstein) or the dissenter (such as Galileo or the hippie)? At what emotional/physical cost do we exclude new ideas from our current world view? Against what assault/invasion are we protecting ourselves? If the lobster could not shed his shell for growth, would there be any lobsters at all? What is the price of poking fun at those persons who insist upon viewing the world from odd angles of vision, whether that process involves turning phrases around in one's mouth, one's ears, one's fingers, one's nose, one's dreams, one's eyes, until one sees with every sense?

Learning modes 25, 50, and 100 years hence may still include the classroom, the counseling center, and other formal structures. But the walls will, indeed, be pushed out to include networks of Toffler's "electronic cottages," television networks we have not even dreamed up yet, "continuing education" networks that make the current ones look like fish weirs constructed by nonliterate peoples. There will be hundreds of thousands of smaller human networks (running beyond friendship circles) that may even be perceived as "re-tribing," one compensation for what inevitably ails the nuclear family and senior citizen compounds. The major subset image for network will be linkage, human linkage. Better that learning be perceived in terms of learners linking with one another than persons occupying chairs in discrete classrooms in discrete courses earning discrete hours and credits or discrete practicum time while fulfilling self-deceiving prophesies and violating most of what we know about human learning! And if we get hooked into developing transcripts for whatever happens in these learning contexts, transcripts for a credentialing society that is still "looking for a sign," then let those of us who believe in developmental learning become creative writers, "narrating" that which was done (by whatever vehicle we must use—picture, computer screen, metaphor, diagram, portfolio) rather than relying upon standardized descriptions of what some school or educator *alleges* to do in Course X, Y, or QQ.

Imagining the Future

"The central issue of our day is whether human beings will develop values that will enhance human growth and hence contribute to social sanity. Growth and sanity relate to the way that values are developed and knowledge is used and the subsequent results which are achieved for our ends, both personal and social. . . .The frontier lies beyond the cerebrum and the aorta; it lies in the processes of self-realization and social reconstruction" (Fairfield, 1971, p. 8).

Teachers and students, as co-learners, need to develop confidence in their ability to use dream images, concoct pictures, concepts, and processes that relate to one another in this rapidly moving world. Shadow images of the future are only faintly visible in the current media displays. Perhaps we can achieve this confidence by moving more boldly *toward* openness, *toward* a sense of fallibility and vulnerability, *toward* daring and ambiguity, *toward* relevance and relating persons, places, and potentialities, *toward* affirmation and continuity, *toward* empathy and loving, *toward* human support and supporting, *toward* "structuring" nonstructure; in short, *toward* a profound appreciation of paradox, irony, and humor. The kaleidoscope may become more valuable than the encyclopedia or dictionary! The evening news programs on television, pervasive fragmentations, provide a handy mirror, since they specialize in and even fondle bits and pieces of information. Who can make sense of the infinite varieties of human experience one encounters every day without sensing, via touch, taste, vision, thought, and intuition, the contradictions and paradoxes of our present universe? Only the paradoxical perspective can reconcile the fact that people are crushed to death while trying to view the Pope, a "man of peace," on his far-flung journeys. And the Holy Father, who claims to represent the mightiest of all Powers, seems powerless to stop the crushing and dying. In the same perspective, the Strategic Air Command, an arm of domestic defense for the United States, proclaims in its motto that "Peace is our Profession." Government presses gobble up forests of timber in order to proclaim the need to conserve natural resources and control environmental destruction. The list of contradictions and paradoxes appears infinite. But how to cope?

Is laughter, indeed, our first and our last, best cope? If we do not laugh at the comic side of life, whatever our personal sense of the comic may be, or find some humor in the human dilemma, what are the likely consequences? What is the social and psychological cost of taking any discipline so seriously that it cannot be put into paradoxical perspective? Can we internalize laughter, paradox, and irony into life-giving, vital attitudes? How do we get beyond the first reflex in reacting to a public disaster and integrate it into our life experience and value orientation in some constructive/active way? And what if we move in the opposite direction, finding ourselves comfortable with self-denigration, corroding cynicism, or bitterness? What then? How does one relate whatever we are learning today, at any level of competence, to the devastating images of a holocaust or a Vietnam, or the scandalous images of a Watergate or an ABscam operation? What personality reconstructions or relocations have these wrought?

Scene: A behavioral scientist of national repute lectures to 155 students in a huge auditorium; she balances pros and cons of the Iranian hostage episode as it relates to the impact of the experience on their personalities; she also considers the pros and cons of solving international conflicts by studying the culture of a people. She leaves the class with the distinct impression that she is "an objective scientist" without an opinion of her own. *Query:* What are the consequences of this pretension of neutrality? *Query:* Is it better to present objectivity as a facade to students, or to present several sides to an issue and then indicate personal biases in the face of facts?

I believe that educators practice self-deception if they espouse objectivity ("Objectivity is what I say it is!"). Educators and administrators of every type must become co-learners, evolving tactics and strategies for wading into both deep and shallow rivers of experience; they must feed curiosity with querying about alternative viewpoints on human valuing, and they must make humor central in learning—wherever, whenever, whatever, whoever, whyever the horizon for doing it. This must become natural, a way of life-learning, and, if need be, it must go beyond the classroom, administrative or professional office, library, or campus, to the wherever the process needs extend. If all the world is a school and we would develop human linkages, let us take seriously the research that has been done by Kenneth Boulding (1956), Fred Polak (1973), Robert Bundy (1976), and others on the human phenomenon that we tend to grow into our images. If this be so, let us eschew images that suggest confined space and opt for open-air images of horizons, rivers, seas, jet streams, and the expansion of human creativity.

References

Boulding, K. *The Image.* Ann Arbor: University of Michigan Press, 1956.
Bundy, R. (Ed.). *Images of the Future.* Buffalo, N.Y.: Prometheus Books, 1976.
Cousins, N. *Anatomy of an Illness.* New York: Norton, 1979.
Dewey, J. *Democracy and Education.* New York: Macmillan, 1916.
Fairfield, R. *Person Centered Graduate Education.* Buffalo, N.Y.: Prometheus Books, 1977.
Fairfield, R. "Learning—Rivers and Nets!" In K. Boulding (Ed.), *Images of the Future.* Buffalo, N.Y.: Prometheus Books, 1976.
Fairfield, R. (Ed.). *Humanistic Frontiers in American Education.* Englewood Cliffs, N.J.: Prentice-Hall, 1971.

Lippman, W. *The Public Philosophy.* London: H. Hamilton, 1955.
McLuhan, M. *The Medium is the Message.* New York: Bantam Books, 1967.
Polak, F. "Responsibilities for the Future." *The Humanist,* 1973, 6, 14-16.
Rogers, C. *Freedom to Learn.* Columbus, Ohio: Merrill, 1969.
Simonton, C., and Simonton, S. *Getting Well Again.* Los Angeles: J. P. Tarcher, 1978.
Toffler, A. *The Third Wave.* New York: Morrow, 1980.
West, J. *Double Discovery.* New York: Harcourt Brace Janovich, 1980.
Whitehead, A. *Science and the Modern World.* New York: Macmillan, 1925.

Roy Fairfield is a creator—he has "imaged" his way from traditional universities to educational innovation as a founding father of the Antioch-Putney Master's Program in Education and The Union Graduate School. He is also a poet, a photographer, a philosopher, a carpenter, a counselor, a humorist, and the editor of Humanistic Frontiers in American Education.

Effective developmental courses require careful planning, stimulating classroom activities, and clear evaluation procedures.

Principles of Design

Jane Fried

The concept of education for human development is probably older than Socrates. Mark Hopkins, on his allegorical log, was educating students for their own development. Whitehead (1949, pp. 11-12) wrote: "The central and controlling concept in education is the living activity of those who study, the kindling of their interest in the process of their personal fulfillment. The teacher himself is an example of this experience, resolutely rejecting the mere presentation of depersonalized information, inanimate conceptions, and thought split from life."

Student-development educators, formerly known as student-personnel workers, did not invent student-development education. However, the knowledge explosion and the establishment of graduate research facilities on undergraduate campuses have led to an atmosphere in which it is easy to split "thought from life." At this time, student-development educators probably know more than any other group on campus about how to reintegrate thought and life, questions about knowledge with questions about meaning. A combination of skills in human relations training, educational assessment, and group-dynamics techniques gives student-development educators the means to (1) design courses that focus exclusively on the developmental concerns of college students and (2) consult with faculty about methods for improving their teaching methods and organization of content.

The split between thought and life is endemic to any university. Student development educators are prone to seeing themselves as "the good guys" who work with the students "where they live," just as faculty often pride themselves on not wanting to get involved in student life, and on teaching facts and concepts only. McCreary (1972, p. 88) has said: "The split between thought and life is found not only in students, but in teachers, administrators, and governing boards. An amateurish delight in the advances of knowledge is often indulged, leaving unaffected areas of belief and action, which, had the knowledge been taken seriously, would have undergone transformation as a result of scrutiny and revision."

Student development education is, first and foremost, about integrating knowledge of the world and human life, with issues of meaning and implications of that knowledge. This is critical on the conceptual, the operational, and the political level. What has been divided for purposes of discussion and investigation must be integrated for purposes of living. When wisdom is separated from knowledge, thought from life, students suffer—and so do faculty and staff.

In the preceding chapter, new images of the teaching/learning process were introduced and explored. After ideas about mugs (containers) and jugs (bigger containers used for pouring liquids into smaller containers) have been broken, or at least put on the shelf, new learning images must replace them: rivers, nets, and waving wheat. When the new images are in place, new methods for teaching and learning must follow. The purpose of this chapter is to describe the design process for developmental courses. The description follows a typical program development cycle: (1) identification of the need for a course or program, (2) organization of the conceptual framework, (3) goal setting, (4) establishment of evaluation criteria, (5) identification of course content, information sequence, and teaching methodology, (6) implementation, (7) evaluation, (8) reporting to sponsoring academic departments, and (9) revision. The first six topics are covered in detail in this chapter. The last three topics are discussed in the final chapter, "Facts, Feelings, and Academic Credit."

New Constructs

Developmental courses are organized around issues that are of concern to college students, not around the subject matter of a particular discipline. David Drum (1980) has suggested three major constructs around which developmental courses may be organized: life skills, life themes, and life transitions. Courses in life skills focus on behavioral skills that are easily described and easily measured, such as active listening, decision making, assertiveness, life and career planning, fair fighting, and so on. The focus is on the acquisition of specific skills to be used in specific circumstances. Skills are learned and practiced in class and applied in real life circumstances.

Courses in life themes are somewhat more general, less skill oriented, and more concept-oriented; for example, identity, sexuality, jealousy, living with others, aloneness, aging. In these courses, the major topic provides the theme. Material used in class comes from a variety of disciplines that can shed light on the theme of the course. In-class exercises and out-of-class assignments encourage students to apply concepts from many disciplines to questions about their lives. "What does this information mean to me and to my community?" is the major question. Watkins (1975, p. 1) has said: "The various disciplines are treated not as separate courses but as different and interrelated approaches to problems . . . [a curriculum may] focus on the individual and address the question "How can each of us be the person s/he would like to be?" Each student answers this question by himself by examining facts and theories from the fields of natural science, social science, sociology, psychology, and communications."

Progress in these courses is more difficult to measure, since each person struggles with the meaning of the facts from a personal point of view. Methods of evaluating achievement in life-theme courses are discussed later in this chapter and in the chapter on evaluation.

Courses in life transitions involve a combination of conceptual learning and skill acquisition. People in transition need to understand the content of the transition they are experiencing (for example, building a marriage, adjusting to college, letting go of children, dissolving a partnership, death and dying, moving through midlife). Information on the general human experience of people in a particular transition is valuable to them. Such information is often comforting, encouraging, and strengthening. It shows students that they are not alone, that they will probably not die of the particular pain of the transition, and that the transition will end. Understanding the entire span of the transition gives students a sense of control and strength. Skill acquisition helps students to make the transition more smoothly. A woman recently widowed needs decision-making skills, self-disclosure skills, financial management or assertiveness skills to learn to control her new life. A person in midlife also needs self-disclosure skills, life and career planning, perhaps journal keeping and some knowledge of how to build a network of human support. In adjusting to college, students probably need improved self-management skills in areas such as assertiveness, study skills, health maintenance, and developing new friendships.

Developmental courses integrate goals for personal growth with goals for learning new information. Evaluation criteria are designed by teacher and student accordingly. *The Journal of College Student Personnel* (1975, p. 336) reports: "Cognitive mastery of knowledge should be integrated with the development of persons along such dimensions as. . . . development of a value system, self-awareness, interpersonal skills, and community responsibility."

An extremely useful construct in the creation of developmental courses is the notion of "affective rationality" (Crookston, 1973, p. 59). Affective rationality is the ability to recognize and understand feelings and translate them into rational action. This is an integrating construct. Facts must be understood if sound decisions are to be made. Too often, in a dualistic world, facts are placed in contradistinction to feelings. Affective rationality identifies feelings as one set of facts to be considered when attempting to understand or solve a problem that is of human concern. The notion of affective rationality permits the introduction of personal issues into a discussion of a general problem.

Since developmental courses are generally problem oriented or issue oriented, students often expect to leave with some sense of what to do next, how to solve the problem, or how to change one's behavior or one's life, based on increased understanding or improved skills. Increased knowledge should be combined with a new depth of understanding, a sense of one's own values, and possibly a sense of one's course of action. In developmental courses, classroom activity moves from the theoretical to the practical and back again. The issue of how to use the insight/information, what it all means, should never be ignored. When performance is evaluated, what students learned and how they applied what they learned are equally important. Facts can be delivered by teacher or student. Guidelines for application can be developed by both. Only students can determine how to apply what they have learned to their personal lives. Evaluation in developmental courses is a collaborative activity that integrates growth with learning goals.

Hybrid Methods

Since developmental education is about integrating facts with feeling and knowledge with meaning, it follows that teaching methods must reflect the best techniques that have been developed for learning about facts, understanding feelings, discovering knowledge, and deriving meaning. The teacher has several roles, and the student takes more responsibility than is typical in other courses. Provoking and supporting meaningful learning for the student is one of the teacher's main roles. The teacher helps to create a structure in which students can define questions that are important to them and develop methods for finding answers to those questions. "Depending on the nature of the relationship with the student, the teacher could be expert, catalyst, critic, facilitator, mediator, consultant, negotiator, counselor, collaborator, and contractor for developmental learning contracts" (Crookston, 1973, pp. 59-60). Methods of inquiry range from library research to on-site interviews to participation in various types of human relations workshops to meditation and withdrawal from others for a period of time.

In class, the teacher's role is often to help the students learn from each other, or learn from their own reactions to classroom dialogue. Knowledge of group dynamics is essential in setting an atmosphere of trust and collaborative learning. In the highly competitive world of the modern university, developing a collaborative, supportive environment in a classroom is a major accomplishment by itself.

As an evaluator, the teacher's role is to communicate personal standards of excellence and to help students define those standards that are mutually acceptable. The teacher helps students learn how to set standards, live up to personally chosen standards, and take responsibility for their own learning. This must be a collaborative process since the teacher is usually responsible to the institution for awarding grades and defending evaluation criteria, if necessary. Finally, the teacher in developmental courses is generally a role model for students. This is especially true in these cases because the content of the course involves deriving meaning out of the facts discussed. If the students are to share personal meaning as part of course content, then faculty must model this behavior and do the same. Students learn from what faculty tell them in class, from what they learn out of class, and from seeing how the faculty member behaves and makes the course content personally meaningful. In the words of the old adage, "Who you are speaks so loudly that I can't hear what you say." This is never more true on a college campus than it is in developmental courses.

Principles of Design for Developmental Courses

Recognize the Need for a Course

This is also known as the "initial burst of enthusiasm." Identify courses or mini-courses around topics that concern students, not around disciplines. Check out these ideas with students. Brainstorm large numbers of ideas with students and colleagues. Remember what you worried about and agonized over when you were in college. Begin with issues that always worry students.

Life Themes. Women in a changing world; men in a changing world; living a healthy life; personal ecology; human sexuality; identifying personal values; jealousy and intimate relationships; becoming a capitalist; becoming a socialist; building alternative communities; the politics of personal commitment; being alone; life/work planning.

Life Skills. Assertiveness; peer counseling; study skills, including reading, outlining, organizing, researching, writing; confrontation; personal decision making; outward-bound courses; wilderness survival; leadership; management of work groups; self-assessment.

Life Transitions. Coming together—marriage or pairing; coming apart—separation and divorce; dealing with loss—physical relocation, death of a loved one, becoming handicapped; new relationships with parents—for young people; new relationships with children—letting go for parents; retirement; mid-life career change; re-entry into the job market or school.

Brainstorm resources that you can generate on a topic: for example, personal experiences; experiences of friends and family; books, movies, plays, music; campus experts; people who know other expert people; community agencies.

Write down all the issues, topics, and questions that you can generate on the theme; share with colleagues whenever possible. Share the idea with members of the teaching faculty, if for no other reason than to get an early sense of "typical" faculty reaction to unorthodox teaching ideas. Collaborate on your initial attempt with another person from the student-affairs staff. This may make you more comfortable and will give you a reliable source of reaction and criticism. Collaborate with academic faculty, if possible. Share ideas with students and solicit their reactions. This is crucial. You are selling a new idea and students are part of the buying public.

Organize a Broad Scheme

Look at the lists you have made and see if any natural order appears to you for using the chosen issues. Shift the order around several times until you find something that fits comfortably with your ideas about the topic. You will be the organizer/facilitator of the learning experience, so the order must be comfortable and logical for you. Ask yourself if the order that you have chosen adapts comfortably to any developmental framework. It may make the most sense to develop a scheme of your own and use constructs from the various developmental theories to illuminate whatever topics you have chosen.

For example, suppose you are working on the theme of "developing autonomy" as defined by Chickering (1969). This can be connected to Rogers's notion of "conditions of worth" (1951), since people who are meeting their own conditions of worth often spend a great deal of energy manipulating others to reaffirm that worthiness. They would be quite dependent on other people for reassurance. Introduce students to the idea of conditions of worth and help them to identify some of their own. Begin some activities by which they can increase their own self-acceptance. As conditions of worth decrease, autonomy will probably increase because students become less dependent on others for good feelings about themselves. Learning to make commitments can also be related to developing autonomy. Opportunities for students to think about and make some commitments can be designed into the work on autonomy, using Perry's (1968) ideas to amplify Chickering's notions on the subject.

Developmental theories can provide a guide to the content alone (Chickering, 1969; Erikson, 1968), or to both the content and the learning process (Maslow, 1954; Perry, 1968; Rogers, 1951), but none of them is all-inclusive and definitive. Each must be used flexibly. In any particular situation, any general theory may be inadequate or inaccurate, and a good practitioner must be able to modify theory to fit the particular reality. To date, the best words used to describe this process are vague and inadequate; success requires a mixture of training, apprenticeship, and intuition. According to Perry (In conversation, 1976): "Don't try to fit students into my theory. Think of the theory as a window through which to view students. The glass is full of imperfections and distortions, so keep moving it around as you watch the students and try to arrive at angles which distort the students least."

Identify Goals for the Course

Cite as clearly as possible what you want to accomplish, what students will learn, and how the course will be taught. Is there any information that all the students should master? Are there any areas that all the students should investigate, even if the specifics of the investigation vary from student to student? Do you want to focus on skill development and leave the content definition more or less to the students? Goals should be clearly identified and made public to the students immediately. The teacher has the power in the eyes of the institution to establish classroom conditions, evaluation standards, and so on. If a teacher pretends that this is not so, or tries to abdicate power, or does not make goals and expectations clear at the beginning of the semester, then that teacher may wind up manipulating the students as the end of the semester draws near. Exam periods and grade sheets seem to precipitate worries about justifying classroom practices, grading practices, and everything else to the academic faculty.

> To state fully the goals of this class would mean to state the individual learning goals of each student as well as the training goals of the teacher. None of us knows all these goals at the present time. The goals of this class can therefore be defined only as the individual learning goals of students become fused with the general training objectives of the teachers. Only through such fusion of purposes will a training climate be established in this class. A medium of support for the learnings which will take place for each and all of us. . . .

One way of stating the overall purpose of this class is that of stimulating and supporting the kinds of learning that are designed to make us more effective members of the various groups and associations in which we live and work. As we see it, the art of effective membership calls for interrelated abilities of three kinds:
1. Ability to diagnose situations
2. Ability to act in these situations appropriately, according to our diagnoses
3. Ability to change and improve situations [From "The Goals of the Class," written by B. B. Crookston for a class in Psychology of Leadership].

Students will develop competence in the following helping skills: attending, reflecting, clarifying, emphathizing, confronting, supporting, and giving and receiving feedback. Students will also participate in discussions about altered states of consciousness, different kinds of life styles, the process of choosing and making decisions about one's own life, the ethics of helping other people make choices in their own life based on their values [From "Course Goals for Peer Counseling," by Jane Fried].

Both sets of goal statements indicate the skills in which the students are expected to develop some competence. Behind these skills is a body of theory that places the skills in a conceptual framework. Theory also provides some explanation of what personal activity is involved in mastering the skills and applying them. Even if the teacher discusses theory only minimally in class, having the theoretical backup and rationale for in-class activities is crucial. If you have a clear idea of the theories on which the course is based, and the relationship of the theory to both the content and process of the class, then explanations and justifications at grading time will be considerably more manageable.

Prepare instructional and behavioral objectives whenever possible. This process has much in common with goal setting as it is practiced in managerial systems like "Management by Objectives." Two manuals for creating instructional objectives are *Preparing Instructional Objectives* (Mager, 1962), which is a self-guided manual with many practice exercises, and *Stating Behavioral Objectives for Classroom Instruction* (Gronlund, 1970), which has several charts and process outlines designed for novices. It is easy to become enslaved to the process of defining behavioral goals and to lose sight of the overall purpose of the developmental course. The goals can be changed, rewritten, reorganized, or eliminated as necessary, but they do provide a map for traversing the fifteen-week semester with some sense of direction and purpose. If you do not know where you are going, how will you know if (or when) you have arrived? How will you evaluate if you do not know what you expected to accomplish?

Teaching the Course

This aspect falls into three subcategories (1) negotiating the terms on which the class is conducted, (2) planning and carrying out the classes, and (3) evaluating the students and the course.

Negotiating Class Terms

The process of conducting a developmental course is built on developing a trusting atmosphere in class. There should be no surprise power plays and few unspoken assumptions about teacher and student behavior. The first stage in opening up negotiations is for the teachers to state their personal goals for the course and any institutional requirements, such as the number of meeting hours expected, and whether or not grades must be turned in. The teacher must make clear any operating standards that students must meet in order to certify that learning has taken place.

The following is a class handout by Jane Fried:

Course Requirements
1) Attendance is crucial due to the laboratory nature of this course. The implications of missing class will be discussed during the first class session. If a student misses more than three classes, his/her grade will be in jeopardy.
2) Three texts are required:
    a) L. Brammer. *The Helping Relationship*, (1973).
    b) D. W. Johnson. *Reaching Out*, (1972).
    c) C. Castenanda. *Journey to Ixtlan*, 1972.
3) Grading is by contract:
    a) *C:* To earn a C for the course, the student must attend class regularly, master the skills presented, and complete a paper entitled "Being and Being With," a personal statement of the student's philosophy of living and helping. The paper must include a discussion of significant life experiences and evidence of at least three outside readings. Students are also expected to keep a journal in order to generate additional material for this paper. The journal will be collected in three parts on March 4, April 7, and May 5.
    b) *B:* To earn a B for the course, the student must complete the requirements for a C and participate in an out-of-class helping project. Examples of such projects include volunteering at the state mental hospital, working as a Big Brother or Big Sister, adopting a grandparent through the senior citizens program, volunteering at the drop-in center or joining the telephone hot-line staff, or keeping a log of helping activities performed in conjunction with the resident assistant position. Students must submit a project report to receive credit.
    c) *A:* To earn an A, the student must complete the requirements above as well as an additional paper on some theoretical problem of living or helping. Topics should be determined in conversation with the instructor.

Note: Contracts for grades above C must be put in writing and discussed with the instructor if the grade is to be guaranteed. People who do not discuss projects and papers with the instructor may not receive credit for their work. Ideas for projects and papers are limited only by the imagination of those involved. Unacceptable work will be returned for improvements. No failures are anticipated.

The second part of the process of negotiating class terms is helping students identify their personal learning goals for the course. This may be difficult since students may never have given the subject of their own learning goals much thought before. They are used to having teachers tell them what to learn and conforming to the teacher's expectations, gambling on "psyching out" the teacher, and hoping for a big win on a paper or a test. One way of identifying students' expectations about the learning process is to use the Student Teacher Interaction Model (STIM). All classes fill it out, including the teacher. The STIM provides valuable information about student expectations for course methodology, teacher behavior, and evaluation criteria. (The STIM is available from the editor of this volume on request.) The results of this informal survey can provide the basis for further discussion of class content and process.

Another system for negotiating is asking students to work in small groups to list learning goals. The teacher also lists goals, and each group appoints a representative to negotiate with the teacher in the process of developing a class learning contract. As part of this process, students may interview the teacher to find out what kinds of skills and resources the teacher has, and vice versa. The students may need a lot of help with this process. The teacher, in addition to being a negotiator, may need to be a clarifier, an empathizer, and a person who helps students translate vague hopes and feelings into concrete learning goals. Excerpts from one such contract appear below.

Sample Learning Contract

The class expects a learning environment that includes the following behavioral norms and skill training:
1) Communication skills—more effective self-expression
2) Empathy skills—knowing when and how to learn, how to help people feel comfortable
3) Self-disclosure and feedback skills—correcting mis-communication when people are on "different wave lengths"
4) Regular reinforcement of skills through practice in class
5) Honesty among participants
6) Self-disclosure from the instructor
7) Structuring of various class activities by instructors; facilitation and direction in class

Class members will share their personal resources with each other, including:
1) Individual experiences with living and helping others

2) Access to outside specialists in areas related to counseling—inviting guest speakers as appropriate

The instructor agrees to meet the learning expectations of the class and expects from the class:
1) Active student involvement in class
2) A comfortable class atmosphere

A final part of this negotiating process is helping students understand the connection between class agreements, learning contracts, and final student evaluations (that is, grades). Contracts for grades and what must be done to earn grades must be clearly arranged with all parties feeling comfortable and able to accept the terms. A significant problem is that of setting quality standards. As in the earlier example, students may attend class, write papers, and participate in required out-of-class activity. They may present evidence that all the agreements have been met, and yet the papers may not be up to the teacher's standard for writing. Topics may receive superficial treatment in the teacher's judgment, or the quality of the student's participation in the out-of-class experience may be questionable. If the teacher is going to reserve judgment on quality standards, the student should know it from the outset. If there is a chance that work which is inadequate from the teacher's point of view will be rejected, the student should know it.

There seems to be no easy solution to this problem, and it sneaks up on the new teacher unawares. The responsibility for grading, setting standards, and being responsible for decisions that affect a student's college record can be very intimidating; often, the impact does not hit until the end of the semester when the final accounting comes and the grade sheet is under the teacher's nose. An effective approach to this problem is to respond to all questions that the students ask about teacher standards and to clarify performance expectations. For example, for the paper "Being and Being With," Fried indicates that she would be very surprised to receive something shorter than five pages, although it is conceivable that somebody could summarize their philosophy of living and helping in five pages. Papers are returned for rewrite if they are substandard. A rewrite is preceded by a thorough discussion of flaws in the paper and always includes a renegotiation of standards on the project.

Planning and Carrying Out the Course

William Perry's (1968) scheme for describing intellectual and ethical development has great utility for the assessment of individual learning style and guidance in the design of classroom activities. Unfortunately, the only way to ensure that all students in a class are at approximately the same level in the Perry scheme is to do individual prediagnoses and to assign students to course sections based on the results. This is expensive and time consuming.

The next best approach to choosing teaching methods is quite pragmatic: Use, at the outset, a variety of approaches to accomplish the goals of the first few classes and try to assess what activities seem to be most thought-provoking, most involving for students, and most conducive to "constructive mismatch." This simply means that the experience presented allows the student to feel comfortable enough to experiment with new ideas and behaviors and uncomfortable enough with old ideas and behaviors to see their inadequacy. Judgment about what is working in the class can be made by the teacher according to the same standards the teacher would use in working with a group: part intuition, part judgment based on theoretical analysis of group process, and part conversation with the group itself.

Use of the STIM can provide insight into the learning needs and expectations of individuals in the group, but the average scores from the STIM may simply provide a norm that applies to no individual. Questions inferred from the Perry scheme are also helpful in prediagnosis; for example, "Looking back over the past year, what stands out for you?"; "What does a person have to do to succeed in college?"; "What things seem most worthwhile to you in life, and why?" Answers to these questions yield some insight into the students' structuring of their own experience, their sense of their relationship to the authorities in the college community, their ability to make commitments, and their awareness of the process by which one carries out commitments. Having a sense of where individuals fall on the Perry continuum is very helpful to the teacher in understanding the student who is having trouble succeeding in class. It can provide guidance for designing specific learning experiences that the student can master.

Planning individual classes is a mini-version of course planning, with much more specificity of method. Specifying the learning goals is followed by the designation of activities that seem conducive to the accomplishment of goals. All classes should include some activity—role plays, student presentation, human relations exercises, small discussion groups; each class should also include some attention to cognition—a summary of what has been learned during the activity, conclusions that can be drawn. Alschuler and Ivey (1973) have identified "internalization" as a goal of what they call "psychological education," a similar phenomenon to developmental instruction. Internalization means that students personalize what they learn. That is, they incorporate their learning into the structure of their daily activities. Their behavior and world view is changed as a result of their experience in the educational activity. Alschuler (1973, p. 609) has identified a learning sequence that maximizes the possibility of internalization:

1. Get the student's attention.
2. Provide a unified, intense experience of the skill, concept, or motive.

3. Develop a clear conceptualization.

4. Relate the learning to other important aspects of the student's life.

5. Get the student to practice in ways that are meaningful and satisfying to him (her).

This is a very powerful way to organize individual classes and groups of classes to achieve learning goals. The system provides a constant reminder of the need to integrate affect and cognition, and awareness of the student's experience and other thoughts and ideas about similar experiences. The format provides a comfortable rhythm for class activities, shifting from action to contemplation and back again. One example of a class plan designed according to this format follows:

Class goals: To discuss and illustrate the Rogerian concept of "conditions of worth" and "self-acceptance."
To help students identify their own conditions of worth.
To practice the skills of self-disclosure and unconditioned positive regard.

1. Attract student attention: Students are given a reading assignment on Rogers's ideas regarding conditions of worth, unconditioned positive regard, and self-acceptance. They also receive a study guide identifying key terms and asking them to identify situations in their own life that illustrate these terms.

2. Provide an experience of the skill, concept, or motive: The teacher explains the Johari Window. Students draw several windows, illustrating their relationships with parents, acquaintances, close friends. They also identify types of information in each sector of the window and relate their conditions of worth to their choice of the kinds of information they shared about themselves with different people. In dyads, each student draws a window that reflects the relationship with the other person. Each one then takes something out of the area that was hidden from the partner and shares it. The listener listens, asks clarifying questions, and makes no judgments. Students then switch roles and repeat the exercise. A discussion of the feelings that accompany the self-disclosure and unconditioned positive regard follows, first in dyads and then in larger groups.

3. Develop a clear conceptualization: Students record their most sincere reaction to the entire process, writing about their conditions of worth, their reaction to unconditioned positive regard, and anything they learn about themselves. The teacher follows with a more detailed discussion of the concept of conditions of worth and the methods by which people can overcome these conditions in their own self-concept.

4. Relate the learning to other parts of the student's life: Use in-class discussion, subsequent journal entries.

5. Practice the behavior and notice the utility of the concept to explain life experiences: Students are asked to think about ways to use self-disclosure; they also look at the kinds of information that they did not typically reveal about themselves and note these observations in their journal.

The summary assignment for this unit, which also included the study of Adler, Maslow, and Transactional Analysis, was to write a discussion of significant life experiences from two theoretical points of view. Use of the Rogerian concepts was one option. The journal was a vehicle through which the students focused attention on their own experiences and which they used in looking for their own life patterns.

The various training manuals on the market for human relations skills generally use a modified version of the Alschuler format. The step that is often left out is step (c) above, "Developing a clear conceptualization." Students may observe a skill, practice a skill, and even discuss how the use of this skill might make their lives more satisfying without ever developing a clear conceptualization about why that skill is effective, how that skill relates to their own notions of living effectively, or how that skill fits into the vast array of other skills that form a large part of the individual personality. Having a general understanding of the principles behind the practice of a particular skill is always useful. In courses for which academic credit is granted, learning the general principles that govern skills and applications is critical to the integrity of the learning process.

Evaluating the Students and the Course

Evaluation completes the circle. Did you do what you set out to do? How do you gather evidence? Standards for evaluating student accomplishment should have been set by contract at the beginning of the course. Evaluating the course itself is somewhat more difficult. An evaluation tool can be developed around the initial behavioral contract between the students and the teacher, asking the students to rate the course on the dimensions outlined in the contract. The STIM can be readministered if the goal was to help students take more responsibility for their own learning.

Students can make their own assessment of the course and its impact on their lives and behavior. The instructor compiles a list of behaviors that were targeted for change or the teaching of skills, and the students assess the impact of the course on each behavior listed. Typical skills might include accepting positive reactions, managing interpersonal conflicts, expressing personal feelings, or listening empathically. An appropriate rating scale might extend from "-3: Unable to do this now under most circumstances" to "+3: Able to do this now under most circumstances." All numbers on a scale should be defined on the rating sheet to minimize misunderstanding. "Yes/No" questions on personal and complex issues seem to make students very angry. The responses seem to come more willingly if the students feel that they have a continuum along which to place answers.

Questions about any dimension of the course can be asked in the semantic differential format (Osgood, 1957). For example, "overall reaction to the course" can be evaluated along dimensions of "useful to useless" on a five- or six-point scale, "interesting to boring," "well-organized to poorly organized," and so forth. Questions about quality of teaching, utility of content or of particular classes, or any other dimension that interests the teacher can also be raised. Open-ended questions also provide a great deal of useful information, even if the data cannot be summarized as succinctly.

In any skill-oriented course, students can demonstrate what they have learned. Audio and videotape recordings of student performance before and after the course provide clear examples of changes in a student's skill level. Any written assessment that was conducted at the beginning of the course can be readministered at the end of the term and progress judged according to the theoretical scheme that informed the questions. The details of several approaches to evaluation are discussed at greater length in the chapter on evaluation later in this volume.

Summary

Designing developmental courses is very similar to designing any training program in human relations. There are two key differences: (1) duration of the program, and (2) extent of conceptualization and theorizing. The design cycle is a familar one: (1) Identify a need for the course/ program; (2) Organize a broad, conceptual framework that gives the course/program intellectual integrity; (3) Set goals for the course on the theoretical and operational levels; (4) Establish evaluation criteria based on course goals; (5) Identify course content, arrange it in proper sequence, and develop appropriate teaching/learning methods; (6) Implement; (7) Evaluate; (8) Provide information from the evaluation to the sponsoring department or departments; and (9) Revise any part of the process as necessary. The dual issues of knowledge and meaning should be present at all points of the design cycle. In any course for academic credit, students should acquire knowledge. In any developmental course, students should examine the implications of the newfound knowledge in their own lives and the lives of others around them. The range of sources from which knowledge is gleaned, the types of teaching/learning methods used, and the content and process of the evaluation criteria should all reflect the integration of the learning process in a developmental course. "The central and controlling concept in education is the living activity of those who study" (Whitehead, 1949, pp. 11-12). Well-designed developmental courses flow from living to studying, from thinking to acting, and from teaching to learning from and by all who participate.

References

Alschuler, A., and Ivey, A. "Internalization: The Outcome of Psychological Education." *The Personnel and Guidance Journal, 1973, 51* (9), 607-610.

Brammer, L. *The Helping Relationship.* Englewood Cliffs, N.J.: Prentice-Hall, 1973.
Castenada, C. *Journey to Ixtlan.* New York: Simon & Schuster, 1972.
Chickering, A. *Education and Identity.* San Francisco: Jossey-Bass, 1969.
Crookston, B. "Education for Human Development." In C. Warnath (Ed.), *New Directions for College Counselors: A Handbook for Redesigning Professional Roles.* San Francisco: Jossey-Bass, 1973.
Drum, D. "Understanding Student Development." In W. Morrill and J. Hurst (Eds.), *Dimensions of Intervention for Student Development.* New York: Wiley, 1980.
Erikson, E. *Identity, Youth and Crisis.* New York: Norton, 1968.
Gronlund, N. *Stating Behavioral Objectives for Classroom Instruction.* New York: Macmillan, 1970.
Johnson, D. *Reaching Out.* Englewood Cliffs, N.J.: Prentice-Hall, 1972.
Journal of College Student Personnel. "A Student Development Model for Student Affairs in Tomorrow's Higher Education." *Journal of College Student Personnel*, 1975, *16* (4), 334-341.
Mager, R. *Preparing Instructional Objectives.* Palo Alto, Calif.: Fearon, 1962.
Maslow, A. *Motivation and Personality.* New York: Harper & Row, 1954.
Maslow, A. *Toward a Psychology of Being.* (2nd ed.) Princeton, N.J.: D. Van Nostrand, 1968.
McCreary, J. *Science and Man's Hope.* Don Mills, Ontario, Canada: Longman Canada Ltd., 1972.
Osgood, C. *The Measurement of Meaning.* Urbana: University of Illinois Press, 1957.
Perry, W. *Forms of Intellectual and Ethical Development in the College Years.* New York: Holt, Rinehart and Winston, 1968.
Rogers, C. *Client Centered Therapy.* Boston: Houghton Mifflin, 1951.
Watkins, N. *Student Handbook, Part I.* Miami, Fla.: Miami-Dade Community College, South Campus, 1975.
Whitehead, A. *The Aims of Education.* New York: Mentor Books, 1949.

Jane Fried is the coordinator of student-development staff training, and research for the Office of Residential Life at the University of Connecticut. She is also an adjunct faculty member of The School of Education. She is the former chairperson of the New Professionals Task Force of the American College Personnel Association and the coordinator of the Burns Crookston Memorial Resource Collection at the University of Connecticut.

Student-development educators are uniquely qualified to help faculty improve their teaching methods and to help students improve their classroom performance.

Instructional Consultation

Deborah Simpson

The average college graduate has spent approximately 2,000 hours in the college classroom. This graduate may have taken one or more courses that focused exclusively on issues of human development, such as those described in the previous chapter. However, the bulk of undergraduate time is typically spent in courses that are oriented around academic content or the development of technical skills. Faculty often have little knowledge of the developmental state of their students (cognitively, emotionally, psychosocially) and teach as if all their students learned in a similar fashion. When college faculty are asked what they expect students to achieve at the end of thirty or forty hours of instruction, a common response is, "I want my students to be able to think about the content they have learned . . . to relate facts and ideas . . . to evaluate results." The concern focuses on thought process and diagnostic skills more than on simple mastery of information.

For students to fulfill these professors' expectations requires both a knowledge of the particular content of the course and the ability to act on that knowledge in certain ways. Many college faculty emphasize the content component of their teaching. However, few of these individuals teach students explicitly how to think about their content. They assume that students already know how to "analyze an argument," what to include in a "discussion of the major themes in a novel," and where to begin when asked to "explain the results obtained in a given experiment." This ability to think about the content—to analyze, to discuss, to explain—varies among students. However, when these same faculty are asked to explain poor student performance, they assume it is due to a lack of knowledge rather than to an inappropriate or inadequate use of this knowledge. Thus, there is a critical need to design instruction that teaches both the subject matter and the skills involved in using this subject matter effectively if faculty are to achieve their instructional goals.

Student-development educators are uniquely qualified to assist faculty in designing instruction that helps students to develop thinking skills as they master information. Grounded in student-development theory, developmental educators can provide professors with new frameworks for understanding the different ways in which students approach academic content. For example, a student's inability to perform well on tests may be construed as evidence of inadequate motivation. After the consultation process described later in this chapter, a professor can come to realize that the problem is not motivation: It is an incompatibility between his teaching style and the student's learning style. Having come to this understanding, the professor can rearrange teaching methods without changing the content in order to help students learn more effectively.

This chapter describes how the unique expertise of student development educators prepares them for the role of instructional consultants. Beginning with a description of a theory of intellectual and ethical development (Perry, 1968), this chapter illustrates how persons trained in student development-education can assist college faculty in designing more effective instruction. This case study is based on an instructional consultation model currently in operation at the University of Minnesota, which utilizes the knowledge and skills of the student-development educator as a curriculum consultant.

A Theory of Intellectual Development

A part of the knowledge base of the student development educator is composed of theories of college student development (Knefelkamp, Widick, and Parker, 1978). These theories provide a way to understand the changes that occur in students during the college years. Of particular interest for purposes of curriculum consultation is the theory of William Perry (1968). Perry's scheme provides an understanding of the changes in the ways students think about knowledge. For example, contrast the student who thinks about the material presented in class only in terms of discovering the right answer for the test with the student who attempts to evaluate the particular point of view expressed by the instructor and decides on a personal point of view as well. Although these two students may have been presented with the same material, the ways in which they think about that material differ dramatically.

Perry's theory provides one way in which the student development educator can help faculty understand the differences between the student who seeks only the facts and the student who seeks to understand several ways in which the facts can be interpreted. Is this difference due to students' content knowledge as some faculty believe? Perry argues, based on his many years of research with Harvard undergraduates, that this difference is due to changes in how students think about knowledge.

The first three of Perry's four main categories are of particular relevance to curriculum consultants. A brief description of each of these three categories follows:

Dualism

In this category, students see themselves as receptacles into which knowledge and truth, as absolute certainties, are poured. Students do not have to question the validity of any of the ideas, factors, truths, rights, and wrongs that they learn because they *are* absolutely certain of their veracity. A response typical of students with this orientation is that it is the teacher's job to tell them what they need to know to pass the test. They assume that the teacher knows all the right answers and that there is a right answer to every question. For movement from this knowledge orientation to occur, the information that the student receives passively must be deliberately broadened so that the inherent uncertainties that exist in the world become more obvious. This information must be presented in such a manner that the student will perceive it as legitimate. This means that new information must come from an authoritative source, the instructor, or a publication, not another student.

Multiplicity

Rather than searching for the one right response (dualist), the individual who perceives the world multiplistically acknowledges a variety of equally legitimate responses or methods for solving a particular problem. These individuals face a particular intellectual difficulty. They are unable to determine which, if any, of these responses is best for a given situation. Thus, they are unable to evaluate and choose between various perspectives to make judgments based on personal values. People with this perspective often consider all points of view equally valid. For example, in this category, students just do not understand how an instructor can tell them their interpretation of a piece of literature is wrong, because "my opinions are as good as anyone else's." For movement from this orientation to occur, instruction must be designed so that students first examine these alternatives and then are forced to select the alternative that seems most appropriate or desirable for the particular situation.

Relativism

The individual in relativism shares the multiplist's view that there are a variety of ways to look at a particular situation, but also recognizes that not all of these perspectives/solutions/alternatives are equally valid in all situations. For the relativist, knowledge is contextual and illuminates differently in different situations. These individuals are capable of viewing the world objectively, of thinking about thought, and of thinking about themselves in the world in which knowledge is uncertain. Decisions are based on a process of reasoned evaluation that utilizes context-dependent criteria to evaluate alternatives. A relativist, when asked to interpret a particular piece of literature, will acknowledge alternative interpretations but will select and cite evidence in support of the most valid alternative. Typically this is the level at which faculty expect students to think about the content of their courses.

However, faculty are frequently faced with students who do not think about content in this fashion. Most college students do not think relativistically. This is especially true during the first two years of college when students typically think about knowledge dualistically. Thus students say, "It is the instructor's job to tell me what I need to know." If these students do acknowledge the multiplicity of the world, it is typically qualified by the comment, "The authorities do not know for certain *yet,* but in time they will." Even if students can live in a multiplistic world, that is, "I do my thing, you do your thing," they often expect more certainty and authority in the classroom.

Perry's scheme of development provides the student-development educator with a way to help faculty reconstrue the problem of poor student performance. If one understands that the students' approaches to knowledge differ among themselves and that these differences form a pattern of development during the college years, then faculty can design courses and utilize teaching methods that are explicitly geared toward developing the students' ability to think relativistically about the world. The student development educator can provide instructors with this knowledge and assist them in utilizing this knowledge in the classroom setting.

The utility of Perry's scheme as a basis for understanding students and designing instruction has been tested in a variety of courses taught by student-development educators in recent years (Knefelkamp's career development course, Knefelkamp's and Widick's literature course, and Widick's and Simpson's history course). Each of the courses has been used to teach both knowledge of a particular discipline and how to think about that knowledge, with promising results. Perry's scheme provides a way to specify both the professor's instructional goals and the students' approaches to knowledge in a form that enables the professor to design instruction.

A Model for Instructional Consultation

The efforts of student development educators to design instruction based on an understanding of the intellectual differences among college students are valuable. However, courses taught by student-development staff can account for only a small portion of the 2,000 hours that college students spend in the classroom. This approach to designing instruction is, at the moment, unique to student development educators. However, the methods have such great potential for encouraging intellectual and ethical development in college students and such utility for helping faculty achieve their instructional goals that they warrant inclusion in the mainstream of academic life on campus. This section will describe a program that for the last six years has attempted to help university faculty design instruction that takes into account the differences among students.

Supported by the Fund for the Improvement of Postsecondary Education and participating colleges, the Teaching Improvement Consultants staff works to provide faculty at the University of Minnesota with individualized, continuing assistance aimed at improving the quality of their instruction. An important aspect of this approach to working with faculty is that it provides the student development educator with a model for instructional consultation that utilizes the educator's knowledge and skill base.

Assumptions of the Model

The basic assumption of the consultation model is that the ways in which a particular instructor thinks about/defines/construes the differences among students will affect how the instructor teaches. Consequently, a major task for the curriculum consultant is to help faculty members broaden their views about students and their interpretations of the behavior of students. Rather than describing students as good or bad, interested or bored (a dualistic mind set), the consultant encourages the instructor to develop alternative ways of understanding the differences among students (moving the instructor toward multiplicity and a more sophisticated understanding of students' thought processes). Typical diagnostic questions are: What is the content? Do "bright" students and "poor" students differ in how they think about the content? How do they differ?

As the instructor begins to broaden this understanding of the differences among students, the consultant needs to broaden the scope of contribution from development theory to teaching strategies, instructional variables, assessment of student learning, instructional design, and so forth. However, the skills needed to stimulate the reconceptualization process are typically possessed by any student development educator who has had training in counseling or consultation and is therefore qualified to serve as a curriculum consultant.

Necessary Skills

Student development educators, as advisors, counselors or programmers, are usually well grounded in basic counseling/communication skills. They have the ability to begin with the concerns of the client as the focus for the consultation: "School just isn't going well"; "The program board meeting was just a disaster." Another skill of the student development educator is the ability to help clients understand their definitions of the particular consultation problems: "What does it mean when you say school is not going well?"; "What happened to make you think the meeting was a disaster?" The ability of the student development educator to begin with the concerns of the client and to understand how the client thinks about that concern enables the educator to *challenge* the client's assumptions: "I think that you are misconstruing the group's responses to your ideas. There may be another way to interpret their response." In this case, the student activities advisor may use information gathered from other sources to challenge the adequacy of the client's perception. Along with the challenges, the educator provides *support* for the client during the consultation process.

The focus of the curricular consultation process is typically defined by the instructor. Time is spent developing an understanding of why the instructor considers certain factors significant in describing the instructional situation or particular instructional problem. During this process, the consultant can gather additional information about the problem by talking with the instructor's students or observing the instructor in teaching. This information is then used to challenge the instructor's conception of the problem and broaden the range of interpretation, while also providing the support needed to maintain the consultative relationship.

Thus the skill base of the student development educator is fairly congruent with the skill base of the curriculum consultant. Student development theory provides the consultant with alternative ways to understand the concerns of the instructor and the behavior of students. These two features of the expertise of the student development educator have been incorporated into the Teaching Improvement Consultation Model utilized by the University of Minnesota. The components of this model will be discussed, emphasizing how the knowledge and skills of the student development educator are utilized in instructional consultation. Each of these components is illustrated by examples drawn from actual efforts in curriculum consultation.

Operational Components

The Teaching Improvement Consultation Model provides faculty with two forms of consultation: individual and group. Individual consultation provides each instructor with the opportunity to discuss, in depth, particular instructional concerns with the consultant. Group consultation provides each instructor with the opportunity to discuss these concerns with four to six other instructors in a regularly scheduled seminar coordinated by the consultant. Both forms of consultation employ information gathered by the consultant through classroom observation, student interviews, and a variety of other sources to clarify the variables that are affecting a particular instructional setting. When used in combination, individual consultation, group consultation, and classroom observation are a powerful means of challenging and supporting instructors' conceptions of the teaching-learning process and the role of student differences in the process.

The purpose of classroom observation (and additional data sources such as student interviews, student performance on examinations, student evaluation, and the knowledge base of the consultant) is to gather information to gain a better understanding of the variables affecting instruction. This information provides the consultant with an understanding of the instructional situation, independent of the instructor's description. Often the consultant is able to observe important features in the instructional setting that may be affecting the teaching-learning process and be unnoticed by the instructor. The decisions as to what type of information will be gathered and how it will be used occurs as part of the consultation process and is illustrated in the following sections.

Individual Consultation

Individual consultation allows the consultant and the instructor to discuss the teaching concerns that are of particular interest to that instructor. There are four major steps in the consultation process: (1) Problem definition and establishing a relationship, (2) gathering data and challenging assumptions, (3) exploration and testing of alternative problem explanations, and (4) evaluation of alternatives.

Problem Definition and Establishing a Relationship. This step involves the establishment of a working relationship between the consultant and instructor through discussion of the instructor's teaching concerns. The consultant must understand the instructor's concerns and be aware of the information that the instructor is using to define problems. "About two thirds of the students are failing my course. The reason—they just aren't motivated"; or, "The students in my discussion sections never discuss . . .

When I ask questions, I'm lucky if I get even a monosyllable... I guess they just don't know the material."

Focusing on the instructional concerns of the professor serves two purposes. First, it helps to build a co-equal, respectful relationship directed toward problem solving. The instructor feels that someone with expertise in the teaching-learning process understands the problems that teachers encounter. Second, it helps the consultant understand the way in which the instructor thinks about teaching, instructional goals, and assumptions about how students learn.

Gathering Data and Challenging Assumptions. Most faculty have a limited understanding of the interactions among such instructional variables as desired outcomes, teaching methods, subject matter, and student characteristics. During step two the consultant and the instructor agree to gather additional information about the problem through classroom observation and student interviews. As stated earlier, this information provides the consultant with an understanding of the additional factors that the instructor may not have included, but could be contributing to the problem.

To return to the instructor whose concern was that students "discussed" in monosyllables, classroom observation provided the consultant with some possible factors contributing to the problem that were not raised by the instructor. An open-ended question such as, "Based on your knowledge, why do you think the experiment yielded these results?" was replaced by a discussion in which the instructor asked specific questions, such as, "Were the results significant?"; or "Did the investigators use a double blind procedure?"

By changing the form in which questions were asked, the instructor made them more comprehensible to the students and thus allowed the students to produce more satisfactory answers.

Or to return to the professor whose explanation for poor performance was that "poor" students were unmotivated—results obtained by interviewing one of the "poor, unmotivated students," as defined by the instructor, challenged this explanation for poor performance. The "poor" student tape recorded all the course lectures and then listened to each tape later in the day to fill in anything she had missed from the lecture. In addition, this student outlined all the readings and then studied both sets of notes for five hours a night for each of the three nights preceding the examination. The instructor agreed that these certainly were not the study habits of an unmotivated student. However, if motivation was not the explanation for poor performance, what was? New evidence allowed the instructor to challenge his own interpretation of student behavior and suggested that the student needed to learn new ways to think about course content.

In these examples, classroom and student data were used to challenge the adequacy of the professor's explanation for the problem in their respective courses. With these data, the consultant and each of these professors were ready to consider alternative interpretations of the problem. The exploration and testing of explanations constitutes the third step in the individual consultation process.

Exploration and Testing of Alternative Explanations to Problems. Using the additional data gathered in step two, professor and consultant propose possible explanations for the professor's problem.

The professor whose "poor" students were obviously not unmotivated agreed that perhaps the students did not know how to think about the material in the manner required for successful performance on the course examination. He stated his new understanding in this way: "I think what we're talking about [the inability of students to think in ways appropriate for the examination] is a good analogy to coaching philosophy; that is, you don't perform well on an exam unless you're trained properly ahead of time."

At step three, the consultant returns to a discussion of the original teaching objectives. They are now connected to the instructor's new understanding of the problem. By thinking of teaching as analogous to coaching, this professor reexamined how he "coached" his students "to think about the content." However, this professor was not sure how to teach students to think in his content area. And, in fact, he was not even sure how his students needed to think to perform successfully on his examinations.

In order for this instructor to teach students how to think about content, he needed to clarify the types of thinking that occurred. As a way to clarify this process, the consultant asked the professor to answer his examination questions as he would like his students to answer. This enabled the consultant to trace the major "thinking" steps used by the professor to solve the examination problems. The consultant and professor then compared these steps with those used by the "poorer" students in the class.

As a result of the comparison, the consultant and professor designed and taught a review session to help students learn how to "think" about the examination questions. This constituted the phase of testing alternative explanations in step three. Whether or not this explanation, as operationalized in the review session, affected student performance positively is decided in step four of the individual consultation process.

Evaluation of Alternatives. An important feature in this model of individual consultation is the ongoing nature of the interaction of the professor with the consultant. The consultation continues after the instructor has developed a new understanding of the problem or has implemented a new form of instruction. The consultant continues to meet with the professor to evaluate the success of attempted solutions. A variety of data sources were used to evaluate the revised explanation that students need to be taught how to think about the content. A comparison of the final examination scores for those individuals who attended the session with those students who did not indicated that students in the review session performed significantly better. The instructor's assessment of the examinations during grading led him to conclude that students in the review session were more organized in approaching and responding to questions. Follow-up interviews of these students indicated that they had approached the examination questions by using the methods learned in the review session. Given this data, this instructor's conclusion was that students do need to be "coached"—to be taught both what they need to know in the area of content and how to think about what they know in order to perform successfully.

The individual consultation process is one means of providing a supportive environment in which the instructor can think about teaching. A second environment for exploring instructional concerns is the faculty seminar.

Group Consultation—The Faculty Seminar

The seminars are typically run in concert with the individual consultation process. In general, the purposes of the seminars are: (1) to expand the instructors' knowledge of differences among students and how these differences affect learning; (2) to examine, critique, and evaluate the teaching process; and (3) to define their teaching goals, with an emphasis on "what it is that students are to learn" rather than focusing exclusively on the content to be taught.

There are several reasons why the faculty seminar is a powerful addition to this consultation model. In contrast to the individual consultation process, the supports and challenges necessary for change are offered and received by all group members rather than by just the consultant and the individual professor. The faculty seminar also provides the consultant with the opportunity to model various instructional techniques that can be used by participants in their own courses. Perhaps the most critical reason for including the seminar in the consultation process can be found in participants' comments. Faculty participants have continually emphasized the importance of the seminars as an opportunity to discuss teaching seriously with their colleagues.

The seminars are designed by the consultant to engage faculty in examining their own assumptions about teaching. Often the topics are based on the common concerns of the participants and are raised by either the participants themselves or the consultant, based on the consultant's knowledge of the issues common to the group members. Thus the data gathered by the consultant during classroom observations can, with the permission of the instructor, be used to examine issues of common concern to the group.

For example, the lack of discussion in seminar classes is typically a concern for many of the group members. This problem was especially important to the instructor whose students responded to questions in monosyllables. By discussing the strengths and weaknesses of discussion groups in the seminar, the participants examined what they expected students to learn. They then decided if those expectations were best met through discussion. Not only did the professor who identified a concern with discussion groups profit from the group discussion, but the other participants in the group also broadened their knowledge about teaching methods and furthered their understanding of their own educational goals.

An additional benefit of the seminar is that the consultant serves as a model. In this particular example, the consultant used a variety of the questioning techniques that may be utilized in discussion groups. The modeling of questions later served as a content focus for the group as participants critiqued the various techniques in terms of their applicability to their own classroom settings. This sharing of participants' experiences and points of view in an environment that concurrently supports and challenges the participants helped these individuals to learn more about the teaching process in general and their own teaching in particular.

The faculty seminar, like any small group, requires a skilled facilitator to help establish an appropriate group atmosphere and norms. The "consultant-as-facilitator" encourages all individuals to participate in order to utilize these individuals as resources for other members of the group. As with the skills needed for individual consultation, the student development educator is typically trained in the area of group development and processing. While the content focus for curriculum consultation differs from that of a student government meeting, the skills necessary to build a cohesive, supportive, and productive group remain the same.

Summary and Conclusion

This chapter has reviewed how the unique combination of knowledge about student development, counseling/communication skills, and small-group skills of the student-development educator can be used to help faculty improve the quality of their instruction. A model for student-development educators as instructional consultants currently in use at the University of Minnesota has been presented as a means to illustrate the transferability and utility of student development knowledge and skills in an academic setting.

The student development educator can use student development theory to present to the course instructor alternative explanations for student performance and behavior in the classroom setting. As an instructional consultant, the student development educator possesses the skills needed to begin the individual consultation with the concerns of the client, to develop an understanding of the client's perception of the problem, and then to challenge those perceptions based on knowledge of differences among students. In addition, the small-group facilitation skills of the student-development educator are directly transferable to the faculty seminar component of the instructional consultation model. This combination of knowledge and skills provides a strong foundation from which the student development educator can begin to help faculty design instruction that includes student differences as a critical variable.

The time has arrived for the student-development educator to move into the classroom. It is ironic that the major impact of college on students is *not* due to the 2,000 hours that they spend in the classroom. However, it is no longer desirable for student development staff to ignore what happens during the 2,000 hours of student life. Student-development educators possess a knowledge and skill base that can be extremely effective in helping faculty design instruction that takes students' differences into account and helps them develop intellectually.

References

Knefelkamp, L., Widick, C., and Parker, C. (Eds.). *New Directions for Student Services: Applying New Developmental Findings*, no 4. San Francisco: Jossey-Bass, 1978.

Perry, W. *Forms of Intellectual and Ethical Development in the College Years.* New York: Holt, Rinehart and Winston, 1968.

Deborah Simpson is a Ph.D. degree candidate at the University of Minnesota at Minneapolis and is associated with that university's Teaching Improvement Consultation Project.

In developmental instruction, student and teacher influence each other and the learning process simultaneously. The teacher must present information, diagnose the communication process, and remove blocks to understanding.

The Learning Dialogue: Teaching

Clyde A. Parker
Jeffrey M. Kreps

There is no concept more central to the student affairs profession than respect for the individual differences of the students. We "cut our teeth" on the fact that students differ in important and significant ways. We pride ourselves on making use of those differences in our work with them—yet it has been extremely difficult to demonstrate effectively the importance of those differences to our faculty colleagues or to define the relations between given student characteristics and particular methods of working with students. Many of us hoped that the extensive research exploring student characteristics and teaching interactions (aptitude treatment interaction) would lead to practical applications. However, reviews of that research (Cronbach and Snow, 1977; Tobias, 1976) have produced the same conclusions: researchers have been unable to demonstrate systematic relationships between teaching methods, student differences, and teaching outcomes. The literature in the counseling field has led to the same conclusion (Glass and Smith, 1976). Hardline theoreticians and researchers have suggested tighter research designs with better controls on significant variables or

This chapter was prepared with support from the Fund for the Improvement of Postsecondary Education.

more careful theoretical selection of critical variables as answers to the puzzle. When extensive research on a particular question does not yield satisfactory results, the problem may not lie in the research methods used. It is often appropriate to reconceptualize the problem completely, to restate the question, rather than continuously redefine the methods by which the answers are sought.

Focus on the Dialogue

We have come to believe that a more radical approach is necessary, that is, a different way to conceptualizing the relationship between students and teachers, counselors, or other student-affairs professionals. This new conception of the process is embodied in the metaphor of the dialogue. The dialogue between two persons about issues that are meaningful to both of them replaces the double monologue in which each attempts to demonstrate mastery of some body of information with no particular awareness of the response that the monologue evokes in the listener. The dialogue requires authenticity of personal response from both teacher and student. The teacher's role is to present information while at the same time attempt to understand the student's point of view and remove any blocks to communication between them. The dialogue requires more than academic knowledge. It also requires that both parties develop an open, nondefensive pattern of communication so that each can be responsive to the concerns of the other. To manage this process effectively, the teacher should have some understanding of a theory of cognitive development or adult learning styles, and a good understanding of patterns of human communication. In addition, the teacher must be able to translate this understanding into verbal communication, through counseling skills. The teacher can then speak in a fashion that the student can comprehend comfortably, diagnose the communication difficulty when the student does not understand or becomes defensive, and acknowledge the student's difficulty or restate the information as necessary.

Cronbach and Snow are the most thoughtful and critical proponents of an analysis of teaching called "aptitude treatment interaction." For them, "An interaction is said to be present when a situation has one effect on one kind of person and a different effect on another" (1977, p. 3). Such a definition is mechanical and appropriate for physics but not for the world of student affairs or other human environments.

Webster's Third International Dictionary defines interaction as "mutual or reciprocal action or influence." In this case the dictionary captures better the dynamic, reciprocal nature of student-affairs work than does the cause-and-effect definition of Cronbach and Snow. Interaction viewed reciprocally captures not only the effect of teacher on student but also the reverse and equally important effect of a student on the instructor. This "student pull," to use Hunt's (1976) term, determines in large part how effective teachers will be in helping a student take the often risky steps necessary for development. Unless we are open to such student influence, we will be wide of the developmental mark in our attempts to assist. Let us explore further why this radical reconceptualization is necessary.

The concepts of both aptitude and treatment take on new meaning when conceived from the perspective of the persons involved in the teaching-learning process. For Cronbach and Snow, aptitude is defined as "any characteristic of a person that forecasts his probability of success under a given treatment," where treatment is defined as "any manipulable variable" (1977, p. 7). For student-development educators, advising, counseling, and teaching are not thought of as "treatment" or as "manipulable variables." Nor is development considered an "effect." Such a mechanical model does not do justice to the human-ness of the persons engaged in the process of development. It is much more meaningful to define aptitude as "any student characteristic that a *thoughtful* counselor, conscious of this characteristic, could respond to in an adaptive way to improve the student's opportunities to develop." Thus, treatment is no longer a manipulable variable, but "an adaptation that a *thoughtful* counselor makes in response to the pull of the student." We have stressed the thoughtfulness of the counselor, advisor, or teacher. Thoughtfulness in this case does not mean "considerate" in the affective sense, which is also part of any good personal interaction, but rather means "consciousness" or "awareness," signifying that assisting with the development of students is done rationally with due consideration of alternatives and consequences. We would emphasize the complex human nature of such developmental interactions in which the student's responsibility to learn is preserved, as is also our responsibility to teach. The important difference is the recognition of the importance of "student pull" and the reciprocal response from the student-development educator.

When such an interaction is conceived as dynamic, continuously changing, and reciprocal, the process of responding becomes very complex. There are no standard responses, no formulas, no universal ways of responding to students in the process of development. Yet the process is not random, chance, or chaotic. The student is potentially a different student as a result of what the teacher does, and, the teacher is different as a result of the student's response. In this dynamic conception, adaptation no longer means simply matching developmental strategies to student stages, tasks, or needs, but also refers to the multiple momentary shifts of teacher behavior in response to an individual student or a group of students, as well as shifts over a long period of time.

The Dialogue in Action

The dialogues that follow are an attempt to illustrate the interaction between teacher and student as described above. In both cases, the thought process/diagnosis of the teacher is shown prior to the teacher's verbal response. It is not possible to illustrate the student's thought process, but the shifts in student thinking can be inferred from the changes in the student's verbal behavior.

Teaching Consultation

As we were preparing this chapter, we were interrupted by a colleague with a situation that can serve as an illustration of the dialogue process. This colleague is a large black male who was a professional football linebacker. He now conducts human relations courses for undergraduate students. In the following example, he is talking about some restructuring of the content and procedures for one of the courses. We have talked with him before about some of the difficulties students have with the content (how white males have and maintain the power in our society), given his size and his being black. He senses that they feel threatened, senses their resistance and their tendency to oversimplify their world, including the issues he wants them to face. In some of our previous conversations, we have discussed procedures he could use with dualistic students (see Simpson, this volume). The dialogue went like this:

Instructor: "We are talking about slavery and this student accused me of not being fair. He said that I should have acknowledged that some of the slaves were treated very well and that in not doing so I didn't present a fair picture."

Consultant: "How did you respond to that?"

Instructor: "I explained to him that this wasn't the question. He was taking a societal question and trying to answer it from an individual point of view. That even if some slaves were treated well, slavery was wrong, and that is why I talked about the mistreatment of the slaves."

Consultant: (Thinking: the problem seems to be one of his not meeting the student where he is. How can I get the instructor to consider the student's point of view as a starting place?) "Have you thought of starting where the student is?"

Instructor:	"That's what I did. I explained to him that it didn't matter if some slaves were treated well; it was slavery that was wrong."
Consultant:	(Thinking: Obviously we have different meanings here or he doesn't want to hear me. I know he knows about dualism—but I don't think that is the problem anyway. The problem seems to be that the student can't bridge the gap from fair treatment within a system to the unfairness of the system. How can I get the instructor to get inside the student's head?) "Sounds like he was having a hard time understanding your point. Any idea why?" [Counseling skills are a valuable part of any consultant's repertoire.]
Instructor:	"I know that students see me as intimidating and they perceive me as having a personal ax to grind. Maybe if I were five feet six and 135 pounds it would help. But being black and big—man, that's heavy!"
Consultant:	(Thinking: That's it. It's not dualism—it's defensiveness. How can he reduce the student's defensiveness so that there isn't the need to reject the concept. What can I suggest that will break down the barrier between them?) "You think it's because he is threatened by you?"
Instructor:	"Yeah, that's it, or the content."
Consultant:	(Thinking: Yes, but you don't want to give up your perception either—so I've got a double job.) "How do you think you can reduce that threat and still get into the student's way of thinking?"
Instructor:	"I see—holding to my point only made him more defensive—I don't know. Any suggestions?"
Consultant:	(Thinking: Now, I've got to stop being abstract and be concrete enough to help him get outside of his way of thinking about this.) "Suppose you created a fiction for him that didn't seem like slavery but really was? One he knew very well; for example, how would he feel about his parents being so good to him that he never wanted to leave home, so that at age forty-five he was still doing the chores around the house and they were still taking care of him. Do you think he could begin to see through the question of human rights, dependency, and freedom then?"
Instructor:	"Oh yeah, now I see what you mean. Agree with him but in a way that forces him to reject his own ideas?"

In the dialogue we found ourselves having to shift our thinking and our responses to take into account what we learned in each exchange about the effect of our questions and suggestions. Not only did the content of our suggestions change, but the ways in which we tried to reach the instructor changed also.

Imbedded in such "reading and flexing" (Hunt, 1976) are some important developmental concepts. We tried to be sensitive to the intellectual level of the student, to his anxiety and defensiveness, and to his white, middle-class culture, as we also tried to be sensitive to what our colleague was saying about his frustration with the student's defensiveness, so that we could help him to see some alternative ways of responding.

Student Consultation

Even though the work of student-affairs professionals spans dyadic counseling conversations, small-group advising, organizational assistance, and administration, the concept of "dialogue" serves as an appropriate metaphor. Dialogue emphasizes the give and take, the challenge and support, of good developmental relationships. It requires that the participants adapt and change as they are exposed to new challenges from the others in the dialogue. A second illustration is taken from an incident that occurred in a dormitory.

One evening some students were having a discussion in the lounge, which turned into an argument. Several women were taking the same course in which the professor had divided the class sessions into two formats: Half the classes were lectures and half were small-group discussions. One student was angry because attendance was consistently higher at the lectures than at the discussion sessions: "As if all you learn is what's written in your notebook about what the prof said, like he was some sort of omniscient God! The students here are sure passive in class." This comment was challenged by another student who said: "Well, the lectures really are more important. All you do in a discussion group is give your opinion and that's not as important as getting the facts straight." One thing led to another and pretty soon some members of the group were criticizing others: "You want to be an English major because you like to sit in the lounge and read novels and then go to class, where all you do is sit around and talk about them." To which another student replied: "Well, that's better than dissecting frogs or watching litmus paper turn colors in the lab; I wonder if you're not part of the lab equipment, you're over there so much."

As we observed this angry exchange that has so rapidly moved from an honest difference of opinion about teaching to character attacks with no appreciation for differences in interests, aptitudes, or values, we begin to search for a base to understand what is happening and from which we might be able to teach the group some important principles of group life.

To begin with, we note the differences in need for structure and organization in learning. This, we think, may be a cognitive developmental difference or a cognitive style difference. Then we note how strongly these differences are evaluated and generalized. It is as though learning from a lecture is morally wrong for some and preferring a discussion group is lazy and slovenly for others. But even more disheartening is that such value differences lead quickly to angry intimidation rather than to interested exploration of the sources and meaning of such differences. We cautiously begin our dialogue:

Consultant: "Hey, I wonder if I can get a word in?" (The group slowly turns and becomes more quiet.) "I'm curious how we suddenly became angry and personal?"

Mary: (She had been mostly quiet throughout, and now reflectively and cautiously offers the following.) "Well, I'm not quite sure, but it seems as though some people like to argue."

Kathy: (She had looked hurt after being attacked.) "I was just standing up for my rights—They were pushing me into a corner."

Consultant: (Thinking: There is more to it than I thought; they probably don't have the skills to defend a personal position without becoming defensive. I wonder, should I stay with the feeling of hurt or move to a discussion of the issues—One more feeling response.) "It really didn't seem like you had any place to go, so you wanted to fight back?"

Kathy: "Yeah, you bet. Sometimes they just keep crowding you until you have no choice."

Consultant: (Thinking: I don't necessarily want to turn this into a T-group. I'd like to help them to gain some appreciation of differences in style and be less judgmental—I'll gamble.) "Is that how others of you feel?" (Heads nod, yes.) "Have you given any *thought* to why that happens and how it can be different?"

Vicki: (Another more quiet participant) "Yes, I've watched this at other times. It seems like very few of us can tolerate an opinion other than our own. We feel so shaky that if someone differs with us we become emotional real soon."

Carol: (She had made the statement about others being part of the lab equipment) "I don't know if it's that bad,

	but we do have trouble if we try to talk about our differences in any depth."
Consultant:	(Thinking: Now it's out on the table. How can I use it profitably? Probably push their *thinking* further.) "Have you given any thought to how it is that people prefer different subject matter or different ways of learning? Maybe if we can understand that we would be less judgmental."
Vicki:	"I've been thinking some about that. You know family differences and all that, but that doesn't do it for me—The issues seem to hinge more on right and wrong. But when I think about that, it doesn't seem to make sense that we can think about one major as right and another wrong, or lectures being the right way—You got any ideas?"
Consultant:	(Thinking: Well, some evidence of thinking beyond dualism—If I take the bait and lay it out, I'll only compound the problem by giving in to the need for structure. I've got to keep them working to uncover the principles, then I'll have a good illustration of both the use of small-group discussion and personal responsibility for learning.)

Space does not allow for a continuance of the dialogue. The process is the same as in a dyad—more complex perhaps—but with "reading and flexing" with the identified needs of the group.

From Dialogue to Personal Theory

We would like to emphasize again the importance of "thoughtfulness." When we began our search for a theory of student development (Parker, 1969) over ten years ago, it was with the hope that we could be more scientific in the practice of student-personnel work. We made good progress with that task in that we were able to identify several theories of student development and relate them to the practice of student-personnel work (Knefelkamp, Widick, and Parker, 1978). However, the application of such theories is not mechanical; it happens in person-to-person interactions like the dialogue. No person can be encapsulated in a theory. Theories are abstractions of what people are really like, so that the most important feature of student-development work is seeing how each individual in each situation is a part of theory and yet more than any theory. Each person *deserves* a "personalized theory." As we enter into a developmental relationship with students, we owe them the dignity of building a theory about them that will enhance our ability to respond to them individually.

Sometimes this happens in an individual dialogue as we attempted to show above. Sometimes it happens in a small group like a planning meeting, a debriefing, or a seminar. Sometimes it happens in an ongoing advisory relationship with an organization. And sometimes it happens in a large meeting, a rally, or an adversarial encounter. The principles are the same in all these circumstances. With our knowledge of how students grow, learn, and develop, we set up a dialogue in which we are receptive to them and their influence, just as we attempt to present ourselves in a way that will encourage their development. Our thoughtfulness in that "mutual or reciprocal action or influence" is what contributes to that "deeper teaching" (Lloyd-Jones and Smith, 1954) that has characterized good student-personnel work from the start.

References

Cronbach, L. J., and Snow, R. E. *Aptitudes and Instructional Methods.* New York: Irvington, 1977.

Glass, G. V., and Smith, M. L. "Meta-analysis of Psychotherapy Outcomes Studies." Paper presented at annual conference of the Society for Psychotherapy Resource, San Diego, California, 1976.

Hunt, D. E. "Teachers' Adaptation: 'Reading' and 'Flexing' to Students." *Journal of Teacher Education*, 1976, *27*, 268-275.

Knefelkamp, L., Widick, C., and Parker, C. A. (Eds.). *New Directions for Student Services: Applying New Developmental Findings*, no 4. San Francisco: Jossey-Bass, 1978.

Lloyd-Jones, E., and Smith, M. R. *Student Personnel Work as Deeper Teaching.* New York: Harper & Row, 1954.

Parker, C. A. "Ashes, Ashes." Paper presented at Twentieth Anniversary of Student Personnel Institute, University of Minnesota, 1969.

Perry, W. *Forms of Intellectual and Ethical Development in the College Years.* New York: Holt, Rinehart and Winston, 1968.

Tobias, S. "Achievement Treatment Interactions." *Review of Educational Research*, 1976, *46* (1), 61-74.

Clyde Parker is a professor of educational psychology at the University of Minnesota, Minneapolis. He has pioneered the use of concepts in student development education in classroom instruction. He is director of Teacher Improvement Consultants at the University of Minnesota.

Jeffrey Kreps is a Ph.D. degree candidate at the University of Minnesota and is associated with Teaching Improvement Consultants.

*Mentoring is perhaps the oldest form
of developmental instruction—an experienced
person teaching a less experienced person by
precept and example.*

The Learning Dialogue: Mentoring

*Virginia Lester
Cynthia Johnson*

The original Mentor was the man to whom Odysseus entrusted the management of his household when Odysseus set sail to conquer Troy. Mentor was Odysseus' wise and trusted friend and counselor. His name has moved into the language as a synonym for any person in whom others have placed their trust. Daniel Levinson (1978) describes mentors as older men who help younger men learn the "ropes" of their working world during a particular period in the young men's lives. These men act as non-parental role models to help the younger people make the transition from children in a parental world to equal participants in the adult community. Women who follow comparable career patterns often develop a similar relationship with an older colleague, if they can find one who is acceptable to them. Women who move from parents' homes to creating homes with their husbands and who do not identify a career path early in their lives tend to see their mothers as their mentors (Scarf, 1980). There is some evidence from research in progress at the University of California, Irvine, that members of different minority groups, handicapped persons, and women need mentors at different times in their lives than do white males. Although the details vary from group to group and individual to individual, one thing is clear: At some time in life, typically during their early twenties, most people search for an older friend, a trusted counselor, a person who can show them the way to adulthood.

Mentoring as an educational process is probably the oldest form of teaching. Apprenticeship is a type of mentoring. A child is choosing a mentor when that child imitates a skilled adult who is doing or being anything that the child wants to do or be. If the adult responds by acknowledging the child's efforts, correcting mistakes, and taking a general interest in the child's learning process, the adult is acting as mentor.

Mentoring has existed in American institutions of higher education since the founding of Harvard College. Harvard was founded for the purpose of educating the leaders of society, gentlemen of the learned professions. A seventeenth-century president of Harvard told his board of overseers, "You shall take care to advance all learning, divine and humane, each and every student who is or will be entrusted to your tutelage, according to their several abilities; and especially to take care that their conduct and manners be honorable and without blame" (Morrison, 1936).

The faculty educated the students in and out of class academically, socially, morally, and professionally. Students were expected to emulate the faculty in all dimensions of their young lives. The integration of in-class learning and out-of-class learning has disintegrated somewhat since the early days of Harvard. Responsibility for academic and professional education generally falls into the faculty realm. Responsibility for overseeing student life in nonacademic areas has fallen to student-affairs staff in most cases. The split between these two professional groups and their general lack of interaction is discussed elsewhere in this volume (Barr and Fried). Currently, campuses are not places where a student can easily find a mentor who is concerned about the student's total development.

What Is Mentoring?

Mentoring as a function of educational institutions can be defined as a one-to-one learning relationship between an older person and a younger person that is based on modeling behavior and extended dialogue between them. Mentoring is a way of individualizing a student's education by allowing or encouraging the student to connect with a college staff member who is experienced in a particular field or set of skills. The relationship has formal and informal aspects. The mentor may be a teacher or an advisor who has been assigned to work with the student and has prescribed responsibilities for overseeing academic work. Activities advisors, directors of residence halls, or supervisors in student labor jobs on campus can also become mentors because of their supervisory or advisory responsibilities. What seems to confirm a mentoring relationship is its informal dimensions, which give greater significance to the contact between the two persons involved. The student must have respect for the mentor as a professional and as a human being who is living a life worthy of that respect. The mentor must care enough about the student to take time to teach, to show, to challenge, and to support. In some elusive fashion, the mentor must embody values, aspirations, wisdom, and strength that the student respects and perhaps wishes to attain as well. In describing his relationship with his mentor, one student commented, "He was the only person I ever knew who could pat you on the back and push you out the door at the same time." This mentor embodied great commitment to his field, great energy in conducting his own research, a serious concern for his students' problems, and limitless confidence that they could overcome whatever challenges they faced in their lives together. Thus, simultaneously, he encouraged with a pat on the back and challenged with a push out the door.

Mentoring benefits students by providing them with role models for personal and professional growth. Mentoring benefits the mentors as well. For individuals who are in their mid thirties and beyond, Erikson notes a need to experience a sense of personal generativity, "a concern for establishing and guiding the next generation" (1968, p. 138). This need extends beyond the guidance of one's own children toward guiding younger persons in one's profession, or remaining creative and productive in one's own work. The alternative to generativity is stagnation. Mentoring occurs whenever experienced people and inexperienced younger people work together, study together, or live together. It is not often built into educational programs on college campuses, although the benefits of doing so are becoming more obvious. Mentoring is a basic form of education for human development because it provides a wholistic, individualized approach to teaching and learning. Students who work with mentors can grow in their own sense of intellectual competence as well as in their sense of purpose, their feelings of autonomy, and their personal integrity (Chickering, 1969, p. 233). Mentors continue to feel a sense of generativity and purposefulness in their roles as teachers, advisors, researchers, and counselors.

Mentor Functions and Training

In a complete mentoring relationship, the mentor performs several functions and guides the student through a series of decision-making processes. Mentors help students to assess their current state of knowledge or skill in a particular area. They also help students establish goals for life and career achievement. Dialogue moves between current knowledge/ skill and future attainment of goals as the student tries to get a realistic sense of what can be achieved and what types of resources and energy will be necessary for the work ahead. Having taken the measure of the student's resources and dreams, mentors, as experts, can easily move into helping a student plan a course of action as the student begins to move toward the goals. At certain points along the way, the student and the mentor will stop and take a look at the progress the student is making. If progress is good and the resources are adequate, this is a comfortable, supportive process. If obstacles have appeared, the mentor can help the student overcome them or work around them. If the obstacles cannot be transcended, then the process moves back a stage or two as goals and resources are reassessed and a new plan devised.

The assessing/planning/acting/evaluating dialogue occurs naturally when an experienced person is guiding a less experienced person over an extended period of time. It is easy to see that the processes by which an academic advisor guides a student through college or a career-planning officer helps a student choose a career path can be superimposed on the "natural" processes to strengthen the effectiveness of the interaction. Any school that uses a student-development transcript (Brown and Citrin, 1977) as part of its advising process has created another natural format in which mentoring relationships can develop.

Training Mentors

As professional understanding of mentoring increases, it becomes obvious that mentors can function more effectively if they are aware of the process described above and have some information about student development. In addition, training in human relations skills and a general orientation to campus resources are valuable. Familiarity with one or more of the current theories of college student development (Perry, 1968; Drum, 1980; Chickering, 1969; Kohlberg, 1969; Loevinger, 1976) will permit mentors to bring a broader understanding of student concerns to the dialogue. Many mentors remember what life was like when they went to college. Many have listened to current student problems and have a good idea of the current stresses and rewards of student life. But few persons on a college campus have a clear understanding of the developmental psychology of the late adolescent/early adult, and fewer still can use that knowledge to develop better insight into the functioning of a particular student who is seeking them out for advice and support. Understanding student-development theory can help mentors feel more competent in their roles and allow them to serve as better-informed advisors to students who are growing through particular developmental and lifestage problems.

Since dialogue is basic to any mentoring relationship, mentors who have been trained in communication and decision-making skills will be more effective partners in the dialogue than untrained mentors. At each stage of the relationship, mentors must be able to listen to students without distorting, to act as a "sounding board," to reflect feelings and summarize content, and to help students clarify values, make decisions, act on those decisions, and evaluate the results of the action. The mentor-training program for Project Synergy at The University of Rhode Island (see Knott and Daher, this volume) includes these elements. The final aspect of mentor training on a college campus should involve some sort of orientation to campus resources and services. Competent professionals who are good listeners can still remain quite ignorant of the services that a particular campus can provide to a student, especially if they work in a highly specialized area away from the mainstream of campus life and have never had reason to use such services.

Mentoring Programs

The concept of mentoring can supply an added dimension to a number of student/faculty or student/staff relationships that exist by mandate. The notion of training mentors can be attractive to staff members who realize that they are already serving in this type of capacity for some students, even though the particular relationship has never been discussed. Mentoring programs exist in many forms on different campuses, and evidence is accumulating that all participants benefit.

External Degree Programs

Official mentoring programs exist in highly organized form in nontraditional or external degree programs. Faculty members help students (1) assess their previous learning, (2) establish personal learning goals, (3) plan an educational program in a manner uniquely tailored to that student's needs and resources, and (4) evaluate the student's progress toward the goals. The faculty mentor and the student write a learning contract that identifies the student's learning goals for a particular project. Together they draw up a list of methods that the students will use to achieve the goals. Together they determine the evaluation criteria that the student must meet to prove that the student has learned or achieved what was stated in the contract. This process is repeated many times during an academic program until the student has earned the desired degree. During the process of creating each individual learning contract, the student and the faculty mentor generally develop a relationship that is more complex and complete than the role-constricted relationship often developed between a traditional faculty member and a traditional student in a traditional classroom. The students must feel comfortable sharing the relevant parts of their lives with the faculty mentor for purposes of conducting an honest assessment of past learning. The process of setting learning goals for a student means helping a student engage in a life/work planning process. This can easily mean that faculty members share what they have learned in the course of their own career development. Helping a student devise ways to achieve learning goals means showing a student how to build a resource network for continuing learning. Setting mutually acceptable evaluation criteria means helping a student articulate personal standards of excellence and achievement. The model of a student/mentor relationship that has emerged from adult degree programs has great relevance to all types of student-development education. For these relationships to be successful, both partners must be authentic, open, and self-disclosing with each other. They learn from each other and about subject matter. In or out of the classroom, this type of mentoring provides a model for good developmental instruction.

Mentoring in Traditional Programs

Mentoring programs also exist on the campuses of the more typical undergraduate institutions. At the University of California, Irvine, minority students are assigned to faculty, staff, or student mentors who have been successful students or have achieved professional success. Students who have student mentors/tutors have achieved higher grades, become more actively involved in student life, served on more student committees, and expressed feelings of greater comfort in the institution. The faculty/staff mentoring program is based on evidence that minority students tend to make ill-informed career choices because of a lack of adult role models in many careers and a resultant lack of information about the types of careers that they might choose. Mentors in this program provide role models of people who are successful in many careers. In the context of a mentoring relationship, students are free to examine many career options and make choices that are satisfying, well-informed, and achievable. The mentor provides challenges to a student's thinking, support for finding the necessary resources, and encouragement for success. Coaches are often mentors for students on their teams. In the ideal situation, a coach is an excellent athlete whose skill the student respects, a part of the student's support system, and a role model for generally effective adult behavior. In situations where the relationships between faculty members who coach and student-affairs departments are good, the coach can help a student achieve success not only on the playing field but also in the classroom and the residential community.

Sororities and fraternities provide a complex mentoring system for initiates. In their attempt to develop the total person, these organizations require not only active membership in the collegiate group but also solid academic achievement and contribution to the broader college community. Older undergraduate members oversee the initiation process of new members, and alumni advisors serve the same purpose for the chapter. Members can look beyond graduation and see people whose lives illustrate the goals and values of their particular organization.

Occasionally, undergraduate students develop mentoring relationships with professors in their major field. This is more likely to happen if the student is involved in research under the teacher's direct supervision and is interested in making a professional commitment to the field. Mutual commitments to a field of interest can easily lead to a long-term dialogue about professional development, choice of graduate school, the social mores of people in that field, and so forth. In the field of student personnel, mentoring relationships often lead directly to career choices, since the field does not exist outside the college community and students are not aware of its existence until they develop close ties to members of the student personnel staff.

Summary

The potential for mentoring exists in many formal and informal student/staff relationships on any campus. The relationship between an experienced mentor and an inexperienced student can provide a model for the ideal type of relationship between any developmental instructor and the students, one that incorporates many dimensions of living and learning and involves mutual respect and concern. A mentor becomes a role model, a guide, a trainer. In many ways, the ideal mentor has the same competencies as the ideal human-development instructor: "Student-centered teaching, training, consulting, and evaluating . . . The student-centered teacher [becomes] the formal guide, advisor, and teacher of the student along the complex journey toward examination of the self, self-others, self-others-group, self-others-community-world, self-nature-society . . . self-life-death" (Crookston, 1973, p. 59). The student-centered teacher who becomes a mentor can help a student through the processes described in *The Future of Student Affairs* (Miller and Prince, 1976), from assessment to goal setting to selection of necessary interventions to evaluation. By use of intentional mentoring, student-development education and developmental instruction can be spread throughout a college or university, augmenting the effect of the student's instructional program. Mentoring provides one approach to help colleges achieve a goal to which most of them aspire—the education of the whole student. In the process of developing training programs for mentors, student-development staff and academic faculty can also build new networks and bridges of mutual understanding and respect. By focusing their efforts on educating the whole student, segments of the professional staff can reintegrate their educational work as well. Mentoring is a process to which all members of the community can contribute and from which all can benefit.

References

Brown, R., and Citrin, R. "The Student Development Transcript: Assumptions, Uses and Formats." *Journal of College Student Personnel.* 1977, *18* (3), 163–168.

Chickering, A. *Education and Identity*. San Francisco: Jossey-Bass, 1969.

Crookston, B. "Education for Human Development." In C. Warnath (Ed.), *New Directions for College Counselors: A Handbook for Redesigning Professional Rules*. San Francisco: Jossey-Bass, 1973.

Drum, D. "Understanding Student Development." In W. Morrill, J. Hurst, and E. Oetting (Eds.), *Dimensions of Intervention for Student Development*. New York: Wiley, 1980.

Erikson, E. *Identity: Youth and Crises*. New York: Norton, 1968.

Kohlberg, L. *Stage and Sequence: The Cognitive-Developmental Approach to Socialization Theory and Research*. Chicago: Rand McNally, 1969.

Levinson, D., Darrow, C., Klein, E., Levinson, M., and McKee, B. *The Seasons of a Man's Life*. New York: Knopf, 1978.

Loevinger, J. *Ego Development: Conceptions and Theories*. San Francisco: Jossey-Bass, 1976.

Miller, T., and Prince, J. *The Future of Student Affairs: A Guide to Student Development for Tomorrow's Higher Education*. San Francisco: Jossey-Bass, 1976.

Morrison, S. E. *Harvard College in the Seventeenth Century*. Cambridge, Mass.: Harvard University Press, 1936.

Perry, W. *Forms of Ethical and Intellectual Development in the College Years*. New York: Holt, Rinehart and Winston, 1968.

Scarf, M. *Unfinished Business: Pressure Points in the Lives of Women*. Garden City, N.Y.: Doubleday, 1980.

Virginia Lester is president of Mary Baldwin College in Staunton, Virginia. She has taken an active role in the planning, implementation, administration, evaluation, and governance of nontraditional programs in public, private, and proprietary schools from kindergarten to the doctoral level since 1952. She is a former dean of Empire State College.

Cynthia Johnson is on the staff of the Career Planning and Placement Center at The University of California at Irvine. She is president of the American College Personnel Association.

*Good evaluation models need not be complicated.
Process and product evaluation contribute to
program success and retention.*

The Learning Dialogue: Evaluation

Timothy Taylor-Gaunder

Sound evaluation methods are extremely important to the long-term success of any program that involves developmental instruction or any other aspect of student-development education. Unfortunately, many developmental instructors whose major interests are in human relations training, counseling, or other "people oriented" activities consider themselves inadequately trained to conduct good evaluations. Evaluation has too much to do with statistics, with precise measurement of small units of behavior, and has trouble accounting for the more elusive dimensions of human emotion. Developmental instructors often care more about how people *feel* than how they behave and sincerely believe that the most important features of human life cannot be measured. These criticisms may well be true, but they do not negate the need for good, appropriate evaluation procedures as part of any developmental program. In an age of diminishing resources in higher education, programs that survive must meet documented needs and achieve their stated objectives to some degree. In developmental instruction, which involves both affective and cognitive dimensions of learning, there is a strong need for evidence that supports the validity of this somewhat unusual approach to education.

The major purpose of any evaluation is to determine whether the program has achieved its objectives. The approach to this question can be either simple or complex. Evaluation measures can be constructed by the people conducting the program or by campus evaluation specialists, or it can be purchased from a commercial publishing house. Typically, some combination of measures is used. The large evaluation question can be broken down into three more precise segments when evaluating a developmental course: (1) Where are the students in the group at this time (cognitively, affectively, in skill development)? (2) Where does the instructor want them to be within a given period of time, that is, what should they learn? (3) What are the conditions for achieving progress in the direction of the desired state, that is, factors that enhance goal attainment? Evaluation should be built into the life cycle of any program or course and should not be a follow-up procedure created shortly before the course is completed.

Types of Evaluation Models

There are five types of evaluation models that can be applied to any course at various stages of its progress: (1) needs assessment, (2) program planning, (3) implementation evaluation, (4) process evaluation—also identified as communicative evaluation or "feedback," (5) product evaluation. These models are applied sequentially as described below:

Needs Assessment. This model answers the question about the students' current level of skill and knowledge and identifies discrepancies between the current knowledge/skill level and the desired levels. After the needs have been determined and priorities attached to them, learning objectives are stated.

Program Planning. This model examines the issue of what the instructor wants the students to learn within a given period of time. A range of potential strategies should be developed at this point to maximize the chances of goal attainment; that is, all students do not learn in the same way, so the instructor should have different methods available for teaching different content or teaching students differently.

Implementation Evaluation. This model should be used during the program to determine if the plan is being carried out as originally described. Does the curriculum correspond to the proposed instructional program. If not, why not? Answers to this second question can be determined by use of the process evaluation.

Process Evaluation. If the curriculum is deviating from that which is planned, the process evaluation will indicate why the deviations are occurring. Process or communicative evaluation involves the gathering of data that may lead to immediate modification of the program, a "midcourse correction." The "Key Features" approach is used in communicative evaluation.

Product Evaluation. This model leads to a final judgment regarding the general worth of the instructional program. Did the students learn what they were expected to learn, change in the desired directions, achieve their educational goals? The product evaluation is typically the one submitted as evidence of what the program did or did not achieve in order to aid the decision makers in retaining, expanding, or eliminating the program.

Evaluation Procedures

In conducting a needs assessment, instructors have several methods available. To measure levels of knowledge, questions that might appear on the final exam can be administered during the first class. This will highlight current areas of ignorance and identify specific learning needs in the topics that the course covers. In courses that have affective objectives, a commercial test that measures the affective dimensions can be administered before and after the semester. Students can be asked to write a statement about why they took the course and what they hope to learn. William Perry's (1968, p. 7) question, "Looking back over the past year, what stands out?" can provide valuable information about what issues are on the students' minds and also about how they think about learning and what they expect in class. Even in a course with a carefully preplanned curriculum, gathering data about the particular needs, affective states, and levels of cognitive development of the students can affect the instructional program—particularly the sequence of information and teaching styles.

After student needs are adequately identified, content focus and teaching methods can be planned to meet those needs, even if the overall curriculum is predetermined. If an assessment based on the Perry scheme of ethical and intellectual development (Perry, 1968) indicates that most students are at levels three and four, teaching methods will involve a high degree of structure. Role plays and experiential learning projects will predominate in class. Students will be expected to examine several points of view about any particular topic and will be challenged to understand viewpoints they do not believe to be true. Within the structure, there will be a high degree of support from the teacher for these efforts and an attempt to build a cohesive classroom atmosphere in recognition of the difficulties the students face and the degree of personal risk involved. If students are functioning predominantly at levels six and seven, instructional methods are far less structured. There are more classroom discussions and an emphasis on helping students to make personal commitments after examining a number of points of view about a topic. Students are more capable of abstract reasoning and understanding different perspectives on an issue. They still require a high degree of support from the instructor and benefit from a comfortable classroom atmosphere. For these students, the risk comes in making personal commitments to a particular point of view in front of their peers. Students at levels three and four need to be challenged to express divergent points of view. Students at levels six and seven need to be challenged to make their commitments known and to share their reasoning and beliefs with others.

Data Gathering and Dialogue

During the course, process evaluation becomes extremely important. Process evaluation involves constant data gathering from both the students and the instructor in order to evaluate the effectiveness of the program. Process evaluation has also been called communicative evaluation because it involves a dialogue between the students and the instructor that answers the question, "How are we doing?" Process evaluation can be described as a series of mini-research cycles focused on key features of the course. A mid-term exam that focuses on cognitive knowledge tells the instructor and the students how well they have learned the information. Instructional modification may be necessary at that point. Administration of the Student-Teacher Interaction Model (see Fried's chapter on design in this volume) tells the student and the instructor how each views the proper role of the other in certain dimensions of classroom behavior, for example, responsibility for determining course content, assignments, structuring the classtime, opening and closing windows, rearranging chairs, and evaluating student progress. Use of this tool tells the student and the instructor what each expects of the other and allows each to modify behavior that diverges too far from the expectations of the other.

Self-Report

There are several other approaches to process evaluation, each of which can be used independently of the others. Self-report measures are effective ways of gauging student opinion and response to a course in progress. Open-ended questions followed by a scaled-response format give students flexibility in responding to complex questions and give the instructor a statistical measure of overall student response (for example, "Is this class interesting or boring? Interesting (1) . . . Boring (6)"; "Is the content relevant to your concerns? Irrelevant (1) . . . Relevant (6)"). An odd number of scale points allows for a neutral stance if the student chooses the middle number; an even number of scale points forces the student to make a directional choice. Peer ratings are a form of self-report in which each student indicates a classmate's level of competence, role in class, and so forth. Examples of peer ratings include: "List the three best leaders in this class."; "List the two most intellectual students."; "Rank order the entire class from most to least participative in discussions." Values clarification inventories can be used to judge the diversity of student values within the class and assess value changes during the course of the semester.

Observational measures include role playing, videotaping, and mentoring. Role playing involves student participation in a structured scenario designed to allow demonstration of skill mastery at a certain level of competence. Role playing can also be done with the aid of videotape, which allows students to observe and critique their own performance as well as that of their peers. These measures are useful during and at the completion of any period of skill training to emphasize student achievements and skill areas that still require practice. Mentoring, in this instance, is similar to an apprenticeship in which a student works with an individual who has a high level of mastery in the skill the student is learning. For example, a student might co-facilitate a personal-growth group with an experienced group leader and contract to spend a certain amount of time discussing group issues with the mentor. At the close of the apprenticeship, the student runs a brief group session, is videotaped, and is graded, in part, on the skills demonstrated during the group session.

Journals and reflective papers are also valuable parts of the process evaluation. Journals provide students an opportunity for contemplating their daily experience, reacting to class activities and assignments, and examining life issues that are relevant to the course. They provide an opportunity for dialogue with the instructor and give the instructor information about student reaction to the class. Journals are usually checked for completion rather than graded for length or content. Reflective papers are somewhat similar to journals, but they focus on a particular theme. They can be assigned before a classroom discussion to provoke student thought on the topic and clarification of personal values related to the issue at hand.

Commercial Tests

In addition to "home-made" evaluation measures, commercially available tests can also be used during process evaluation and product or summary evaluation. A number of published, validated tests that can be correlated with various theories of student development can be found in the source books listed at the close of this chapter. Advantages to the use of published tests includes the availability of test reviews by the author and other critics who discuss the test's reliability and validity checks. Commercial tests provide safeguards against the teacher's nonobjectivity and student bias. Computer-scoring services, professional interpretation of test results, and information about national norms on the test are also often available to test users. In the use of recent tests, authors are generally willing to discuss the results of administration of the test with a particular population in exchange for contribution of the results to the author's data base.

Some of the constraints on the use of published tests include the cost of purchase and scoring, time delays in mailing and processing of computerized scores, and the incompatibility of test content with some course objectives. The issue of the instructor's resistance to formal testing and the associated inadequacy felt by many instructors at interpreting sophisticated test results may also be significant. Goldman (1971) makes an interesting observation about reliability constraints of current tests. These tests are constructed to have high reliability, that is, relative stability over time. This enhances a high predictive ability for the tests. In the case of developmental instruction, however, learning is meant to produce change during relatively short periods. Therefore, "the selection of less stable tests may be more appropriate" (p. 445).

Ideally, commercial tests can be used in combination with locally developed tests to help validate the instructor's measures as well as gather data on student performance and change. When a locally developed test is administered at the same time as a commercial test that measures the same variables, the results of the two tests can be correlated statistically. If the correlation between the two sets of test results is positive, it can be assumed that the homemade test has a degree of validity beyond face and expert validity indicators. The following simple guidelines are basic to the construction of any valid test: (1) The test should be easy to read and understand, neat, and accompanied by clear instructions; (2) Every effort should be made to pilot the test with a representative group of students. The data collected can be fed back into test improvement before the next administration; (3) Experts in the field should be given copies of the model test for review of content accuracy and comprehensibility.

A Case Study

A case study that illustrates both process and product evaluation follows. This example summarizes several of the steps presented in the material above and illustrates the evaluation process. The program presented in this study is an empathy training model for peer counselors in a crisis intervention center. Instructor teams were assigned to groups of student volunteers. The program's objectives were to train the students in the skills of empathic responding so that they reached a certain level of competence, and to staff the center with the student counselors who achieved that level. Students who did not achieve the level became members of the student administrative staff. The training program involved five structured learning modules. Each module included a didactic presentation on empathic listening and an experiential component of practice exercises.

The evaluation of the program asked the following question: Were the students who scored high on empathy skills and who were also well liked by their instructors more likely to be assigned to the counseling staff or the administrative staff? Several evaluation measures were used. Students and instructors filled out an "empathy check list" geared to the five levels of training. Questions included: (1) How well did the student identify feeling words in a taped problem? (2) How well did the student discriminate between empathic and non-empathic examples? (3) Was the student able to write a minimally empathic response to a stated problem? (4) Did the student exhibit a range of personal feelings in response to a taped statement? (5) Can the student deliver an empathic response in a live, role-play situation? These questions were scored on a weighted scale from "Unsatisfactory" to "Highly Satisfactory," with a one-through-seven range. Instructors were asked how well they liked each student at the end of each module and at the end of the program, for example, "How well did you like/care for this student?" Responses were distributed on a seven-point scale from "not at all" to "very much." The FIRO-B (Schutz, 1978), a test that measures a person's ability to express affection, was correlated with the instructor's liking scale. The final product evaluation compared the instructor's liking scores, FIRO-B scores, and empathy scores for students in both groups—the counseling and the administrative staffs. High empathy skills were expected to be the discriminating variable between the two groups, indicating that students were chosen for the counseling staff based on their skill, not on their attractiveness to the instructors.

Summary

From this brief overview of evaluation methods and models, it should be clear that evaluation is a manageable task for developmental instructors. Test construction and other measurement techniques are not necessarily complicated or mysterious. Effective use of process evaluation can increase student motivation by giving students a strong sense of their own ability to improve. Any course objective can be measured by labeling skills, emotions, values, and knowledge associated with achievement of the objective and assigning a numerical continuum to it. Objectivity in most areas of developmental instruction is elusive, if not impossible, to achieve. However, through the use of proven evaluation methods, a reasonable portrait of student progress can be drawn statistically. And if the portrait appears to be numerically monochromatic rather than multicolored, emotional, and human, it is still an accurate if rather limited portrait. Program planners and those who make budget decisions will probably be pleased to have the opportunity to look it over.

References

Anastasi, A. *Psychological Testing.* New York: Macmillan, 1976.
Asher, J. *Educational Research and Evaluation Methods.* Boston: Little, Brown, 1976.

Buros, O. *Personality Tests and Reviews.* Highland Park, N.J.: Gryphon Press, 1970.
Buros, O. *Mental Measurement Yearbook.* Highland Park, N.J.: Gryphon Press, 1978.
Chun, K., Cobbs, I., and French, R. *Measures for Psychological Assessment.* Ann Arbor, Mich.: Institute of Social Research, 1975.
Goldman, L. *Using Tests in Counseling.* Santa Monica, Calif.: Goodyear, 1971.
Perry, W. *Forms of Ethical and Intellectual Development in the College Years.* New York: Holt, Rinehart and Winston, 1968.
Schmuck, R., and Schmuck, P. *Group Processes in the Classroom.* Dubuque, Iowa: William C. Brown, 1979.
Schutz, W. *FIRO Awareness Scales Manual.* Palo Alto, Calif.: Consulting Psychologists Press, 1978.

Timothy Taylor-Gaunder holds a master's degree in educational psychology from the University of Connecticut. He is currently employed as a planning analyst for the state of Connecticut and has worked at the Institute for Social Inquiry, University of Connecticut.

Project Synergy helps freshmen to develop college survival skills, improved interpersonal skills, and a clearer sense of themselves as emerging adults.

Project Synergy

J. Eugene Knott
Douglas Daher

University students are often academically prepared for careers but inadequately grounded in some basic life skills. A comprehensive, internal evaluation conducted at the University of Rhode Island indicated that undergraduates were receiving satisfactory instruction in most academic disciplines; however, many demonstrated minimal competence for the more pervasive demands of general living. These include such skills as decision making, coping with stress, managing one's physical and emotional maturation, as well as developing a broad range of interpersonal and social abilities. The need for life-skill education is not confined to the University of Rhode Island. Numerous reports have shown that the more practical processes of acquiring life skills in addition to academic knowledge is a major need felt by recent college graduates. Specialization and the enormous growth of the body of knowledge that is available for study have also contributed to a climate in which teaching life skills can be viewed as an ill-afforded luxury in the curriculum.

Project Synergy is an undergraduate and graduate program. Nearly three hundred students and twenty-seven faculty and staff members have participated in the program. Four courses have been adopted in the curriculum, and a program evaluation is in process. These efforts have been part of a novel strategy for providing life-skill and developmental instruction.

Project Synergy has three components: instruction, mentoring, and evaluation. The objectives of this program are:
1. To develop, refine, and assess new approaches to life-skill education.
2. To implement courses that deal with the developmental concerns of students in cognitive, intrapersonal, and social aspects of their lives. New instructional methods are used in these courses.
3. To augment the learning process by providing mentors for the students.
4. To measure developmental changes and to research the effects of the Synergy experience.

For undergraduates, two courses have been implemented. A third course is now being formulated.

The teaching program evolved from three primary sources: (1) A needs assessment conducted with the University of Rhode Island freshmen. Course themes were developed while keeping the needs of the freshmen in mind. Student needs were typical of those described in other literature on the topic of college student development; (2) A multidimensional model of student development, which projects student needs and learning styles (Drum, 1980); and (3) A growing body of literature on "deliberate psychological education."

This provided the content orientation for the preparation and application of the mentor role and the corresponding graduate courses. More will be said of that later.

The topical outline of the undergraduate courses is given below:

Course Number 1: Personal Development

Modes of Human Development
Mapping Skills
Problem-Solving Skills
Developmental Competencies
Academic Learning Skills
Physical Well-Being
Human Sexuality
Coping with Stress and Anxiety
Interpersonal Behavior
Negotiation and Assertion Skills
Developmental Synthesis

Course Number 2: Toward Self-Understanding

Modes of Human Development
Self-Worth and Self-Defeating Behaviors
Ego Loss and Mood Depression

Loneliness and Loss
Meanings of Death
Impacts of Sex-Role Stereotyping
Love, Intimacy, and Jealousy
Relationship Enhancement
Decision-Making Skills
Career and Life Direction
Developmental Synthesis

Course Number 3: Perspectives on Being

Perspectives on Being
  Me (Self-Awareness)
  Male/Female (Sex, Gender, and Role Issues)
  Black, Red, White, Yellow (Racial Awareness)
  In the Community (Habitat Focus)
  In the Nation (National Focus)
  In the World (International Focus)
  In the Universe (Cosmological Views)
  In the Future (Humanity Projected)
Developmental Synthesis

Instruction

Teaching methods for these courses are primarily experiential. Students are expected to be actively involved in the learning process, and the classes are structured accordingly. The courses meet for seventy-five minutes twice weekly. They are taught by teams who draw on a core of student-development educators and several topical lecturers. Classes are held in settings that allow for easy use of open spaces, physical movement, and small-group activities. Each thematic unit involves a didactic segment and an experiential segment. Students are exposed to conceptual information and given the opportunity to apply what they have learned in structured exercises. The conceptual base and methodology of structured groups (Drum and Knott, 1977) is applied in the construction of most teaching units.

"Modes of Human Development" constitutes the first unit of the first and second courses. Students are asked to respond to a series of questions designed to provoke self-analysis and reflection. On completion of the questions, students learn about the model of human development that provides the basis for the course and are asked to fit themselves into the developmental scheme. They reflect on their ideas about themselves, the way they think, and their patterns of interaction with others. As they become more conscious of their own behavior and developmental patterns, they are more capable of examining the long-term consequences of current behavior (for a different approach to the same phenomenon, see Weinstein, this volume), and changing that behavior if they wish. For example, if students begin to realize that their criteria for moral reasoning have been highly dependent on limited external sources, then they have the opportunity to begin observing their own moral judgments in daily activity and evaluating the impact of those judgments on the rest of their lives. Without such awareness, the students would proceed blindly.

The units on skills and themes are intended to resolve discrete behavioral and attitudinal issues in their respective topic areas. These units are sequentially ordered to enhance their concurrence with the types of student experiences frequently encountered during various phases of a semester. For example, "Mapping Skills" is taught early in the first semester when new students are still trying to understand their new environment and learn how to function in it. "Study Skills" comes closer to mid-terms.

In "Developmental Synthesis," which closes all three courses, all the conceptual elements of each course are drawn together. Students are encouraged to identify the various aspects of their lives that have contributed to their own change and growth. They examine changes in their own self-awareness and their awareness of their relationships with others and set personal learning objectives for the future.

Mentoring

In addition to class meetings, students have hour-long sessions with their graduate student or faculty mentor each week. Mentoring involves dealing with individuals across the entire range of human needs in order to advise, counsel, or guide them (Breen, Donlon, and Whitaker, 1975). Mentor groups are limited to four or five students and are intended to provide an informal and supportive atmosphere in which students can apply course information to the circumstances of their own lives. In addition to group mentoring sessions, students meet individually with their mentors twice each semester, correspond with their mentors in written or taped personal journals that are exchanged weekly, and write personal reflections after each topical unit has been completed. The majority of the final synthesis unit is conducted in mentor groups.

The graduate students who function as mentors participate in a year-long, six-credit seminar in developmental counseling, which has three major objectives:
1. To examine developmental theory, focusing particularly on the adolescent-to-young-adult transformation period.
2. To learn, apply, and refine the component behaviors entailed in the role of mentor/developmental counselor, for example, listening, guiding conversation, responding, suggesting approaches to problems.

3. To articulate components of Synergy in working with the undergraduate students, for example, integrating content and skill training, and assisting in the evaluation process.

Graduate students are also assigned a supervisor from the faculty to whom they submit weekly journals and with whom they confer periodically on an individual basis. Some members of Synergy's core of student-development educators have elected to serve as mentors for undergraduate groups in addition to their work with graduate students.

Supplementing Synergy's instructional and mentoring phases are a series of optional social activities, such as plays, outings, and so forth, which provide opportunities to share in common experiences less defined by academic boundaries. In its initial years, Synergy arranged for participants to live in the same residential unit and utilized the common living space as the site of coursework as well as much of the socialization aspect. A common residence has not proved essential to the achievement of Synergy's developmental objectives, and such a residential requirement has occasionally been a disadvantage. Students who live in other halls were not permitted to enroll in Synergy. Commuters were excluded for the same reason. Thus, enrollment is no longer restricted by residence.

Evaluation

The assessment of undergraduate learning in Synergy is based on a modified form of "contingency contracting." Students are provided with the contract during the first class and are given examples of different contingency outcomes. The contract consists of three sections, each of which influences the student's grade differently. Section One is contingent upon participative attendance, requiring attendance at a minimum number of classes and mentoring sessions in order to achieve the desired grade. This is vital to the program's heavily experiential methodology. Section Two represents the core of the contract. The four major requirements are: (1) Content packages for each skill or theme unit, which includes all assigned written tasks and a reflective statement on the unit's content and text readings. These packages are evaluated by the student development educator who teaches the particular unit; (2) Personal development journals submitted weekly to the mentors. Developmental influence and movement by the student are recognized; (3) Special projects (for example, Career Directions Informational Interviews Project) or literature reviews; and (4) A major term assignment on self-development, which is written at the conclusion of the course. These four requirements are each weighted differentially (3.0, 2.5, 1.5, and 3.0, respectively) and multiplied by the standard points assigned to the letter grades. Point ranges for achieving a final grade are charted out on the contract. Evaluation of student material is not dependent upon rate or level of development (if any), but rather on how able the students have been in reflecting upon what has happened to them. Two steps backwards, understood and articulated clearly, would grade higher than one step forward that was not acknowledged by the student. Section Three of the contract requires student participation in the pre/post assessment battery, and incompleted assessments result in withheld grades.

There are two major elements in Synergy's assessment scheme: developmental process and individual behavioral changes. The developmental assessment involves the measurement of developmental levels and positions within the "cognitive," "interpersonal," and "social" areas. The progress of students on these three developmental dimensions is assessed at several points in the course of the program. Instrumentation includes measures of ego development, reasoning abilities, learning styles, demographic and sociostructural factors, self-esteem, perceived locus of control, life events and stressors, physical health, and psychological well-being. All involve measures that have been previously standardized or devised specifically for Synergy. In addition, a structured interview process has been used with first-year participants during their subsequent year to acquire supplemental data. Lastly, a two-part course evaluation system has been tested successfully in Synergy. This entails both immediate, individual, subjective evaluation of each class session using a simple, two-part, three-dimensional rating scale, followed by the employment of a post-hoc course evaluation device called SET, or "Student Evaluation of Teaching." The comprehensive assessment scheme is linked to the developmental model that the students receive in the beginning of the semester. Thus, the merits of Project Synergy can be examined in terms of both the impact it has on student development and the success and satisfaction experienced by those students. Data are presently being analyzed, and we are awaiting further funding for additional analysis and interpretation. A conviction borne of our efforts to date in Synergy and reinforced from speaking with educators from other experiments in developmental education in postsecondary settings is that the reflective synthesis required of students as they attempt to chart and monitor their own multifaceted maturational process is a major, necessary ingredient to the long-term efficacy of this type of approach to developmental instruction.

Assessment of individual behavioral change is literally the measurement of movement on variables specifically treated in the instructional process. These are typically measured in a pre-test/post-test fashion used immediately after the course is completed and again at later intervals to determine persistence of changes. The three major dimensions of change evaluated therein are categorized as Interpersonal Skills, Intrapersonal Themes, and Life Transitions. Some measures are self-reported, others involve paper-and-pencil inventories, while some are rater-observed. These measures are also accomplished by using mostly standardized materials with some locally devised instrumentation, involving fourteen measures altogether.

Program Value

There are a number of intangibles about the atmosphere encompassing Project Synergy that probably influence the generally high level of student involvement and satisfaction. The amount of time the students are afforded in small groups is greater and personal contact with the Synergy staff is more mutually responsive than what many other courses offer, especially for first- and second-year students. Such contact facilitates a sense of commitment toward the course, particularly when the students observe the time and energy invested by others in their own developmental potential. Likewise, the expectation that the majority of learning within Synergy will be accomplished through "active modalities" heightens the level of shared responsibility for skill acquisition and theme exploration. The format of partial-contingency contracting for evaluation allows the students flexibility, which gives them a measure of true control over their eventual grade, and they recognize their role in determining personal learning outcomes. The relevance of the course content to their immediate experiences and needs also seems to contribute to student involvement.

Early resistance to incorporation of such course content was encountered from curriculum oversight committees of faculty. This resistance evaporated once the impact and import of Synergy's objectives were experienced. Initial reservations were mainly stated as concern over the "orientation"—like the quality of some topics. Once skeptical faculty were actively involved, however, a radical transformation occurred, with the program's original detractors becoming its most outspoken advocates. In summary, Synergy is designed to promote intentional cognitive and behavioral changes in undergraduate students and graduate mentors by creating an environment for self-exploration and growth, and by enabling a synthesis of that developmental movement. We have been fortunate thus far in realizing those goals beyond even our initial hopes, although it is clearly an area worthy of more attention and development in the spirit of promoting a primary learning process.

References

Breen, P., Donlon, T., and Whitaker, U. "The Learning and Assessment of Interpersonal Skills," Cooperative Assessment of Experiential Learning working papers, #4 and #5. Princeton, N.J.: Educational Testing Service, 1975.
Drum, D. "Understanding the student: The input variable in education." In J. Hurst and W. Morrill (Eds.), *Dimensions of Intervention for Student Development.* New York: Wiley, 1980.

Drum, D. J., and Knott, J. E. *Structured Groups for Facilitating Development: Acquiring Life Skills, Resolving Life Themes and Making Life Transitions.* New York: Human Sciences Press, 1977.

Gene Knott is the associate director of the Office of Counseling and Student Development at the University of Rhode Island. He is also an adjunct professor of psychology, counseling, and family studies. His major areas of interest are in structured groups for psychological education and death and bereavement counseling.

Doug Daher is a staff psychologist at Cowell Student Health Center, Stanford University. He was the coordinator of the National Clearinghouse for Structured Group Programs at the University of Rhode Island. His special interests are in the area of spiritual issues in psychology and jealousy.

*"Education of the Self" is a course that provides
students with a setting, time, and structure, including
emotional support from faculty and peers, to
increase their self-knowledge.*

Self-Science Education

Gerald Weinstein

For the past eleven years a course entitled "Education of the Self" has been taught to graduate and undergraduate students at the University of Massachusetts. The course has never failed to be overenrolled. It is so popular because it is one of the few places in an academic setting where students are provided with a setting, time, and structure with psychological support and guidance to conduct an intensive inquiry into certain aspects of themselves; they can treat themselves as the subject of inquiry with the goal of increasing their self-knowledge. Students gain all this plus three credits. It is one of the few times in their formal educational career when they get academic credit for learning about who they are.

Goals and Format

The class (usually between thirty and forty students) meets for three hours once a week for fifteen weeks. Students are expected:
1. To observe and make an inventory of certain aspects of their own internal responses and external behaviors and clearly identify their patterns of response.
2. To elaborate on both the positive and negative consequences of particular response patterns.
3. To identify the personal/social history of certain of their response patterns.

4. To design and implement experiments on uncomfortable or ineffective response patterns to see if such experiments yield more positive consequences (these response patterns are termed "dissonant").
5. To evaluate and choose alternative responses to personally dissonant situations.
6. To utilize various cognitive/affective models for "tracking" and "treating" dissonant patterns.

The course is presented in two major phases. In the first phase (about one half the semester), a variety of cognitive models are presented, such as "The Trumpet" (to be described in greater deail), "Aspects of Transactional Analysis," "Gestalt Therapy," "Re-evaluation Counseling," and "Behavioral Therapy." Accompanying the introduction of each of these models are a series of experiential, structured exercises that provide the data to be analyzed according to the various models and theories. The purpose of the models is to provide the students with systematic strategies for understanding their responses to a variety of situations.

During the second phase of the course, the class is divided into three-person work groups. Each member selects a dissonant pattern and works on that pattern by utilizing the various models and analytical tools presented in the first phase. The group members act in supportive and clarifying roles for each other.

The Trumpet

The major organizer of the course is a problem-solving model known as "The Trumpet." The trumpet is a metaphorical symbol depicting a restricted input (the mouthpiece) to an elaborated output (the bell). The student begins at the restricted end of the trumpet process by choosing to confront some dissonant pattern. The student then moves through the steps described below, identifying the response pattern, clarifying understanding of the behavior and its implications, and then transforming it into a more satisfying pattern. These steps will now be described in some detail in order to provide the reader with a general idea about what actually takes place during the course.

Confrontation. The confrontation is the basic experience that is explored in detail. The experience is derived from either a planned structured exercise, that is, fantasy, simulation, game, and so forth, or some experience of an actual life event, such as "the last time you made an important decision."

Making an Inventory. At this point in the process, students examine their responses to a particular confrontation by reflecting on and recording the sequence of behaviors, thoughts, feelings, and sensations that occurred

as they responded to the confrontation. They seek to answer such questions as:
- What did I do?
- What specific actions or "non-actions" did I demonstrate?
- What was my body-language, my facial expression, communicating?
- What sentences, monologues, or dialogues were going through my mind?
- What were the judgments I was making?
- What feelings did I experience? How intense were they?

By constantly practicing such questioning, students hope to increase their skills in naming and differentiating their response to different situations. They are beginning to become "self-scientists," people who can observe, label, and evaluate their own behavioral problems and change them appropriately.

Pattern Identification. Once their responses are inventoried as completely as possible, the task for the students is to determine in what ways their responses were typical or consistent with their responses to similar situations. Some questions raised are:
- Do I recognize anything habitual in the responses I just demonstrated?
- Does my set of responses remind me of my responses to other situations?
- What kinds of situations usually stimulate this particular set of responses in me?

Patterns are named in the following form:

Whenever I'm in a situation where (conditions) ____ , ____ , etc., I usually (behaviors) ____ , ____ , ____ . I experience feelings of ____ , ____ , ____ . The sentences that pass through my mind are ____ , ____ , ____ .

To illustrate the process clearly, we will take an example from one of the students and process it through the remaining steps. Her pattern, as she described it, was: "Whenever I'm in a situation in an academic classroom and there is an open discussion where everyone is expressing their opinions, I begin to experience feelings of nervousness, fright, and anxiety. This becomes more pronounced when I have something to say. My heart starts pounding and my chest feels constricted. The voices in my head are saying 'go ahead and tell them.' But a much stronger voice says 'Better not! Why take a chance? Everybody here seems to know what they're talking about. Suppose you say something stupid?' And so I sit there and don't do anything except try to look calm and wise. Afterwards I feel angry at myself for being so timid."

After the pattern has been named and clarified, students trace the history of the pattern. This history includes their earliest memories of responding this way, how the pattern manifested itself during the different stages of the person's life, and what seemed to be some antecedents to this particular style of response. The task at this phase of the trumpet process is not to explain or interpret the pattern, but to *describe* it from as many perspectives as possible.

Identifying patterns of internal and external responses in one's life necessitates a complex set of skills. While most students manage to classify and group aspects of external phenomena rather easily, quite often they require a good deal of guidance and practice in observing and describing their own patterns of behavior.

Function. Students are now directed to determine what purposes their pattern serves. They are guided through a series of questions and techniques to see what the patterned responses help them *get* and what it helps them *avoid*. In our example, the function of the responses involved in her nonparticipation in class discussions was described as: "Not talking in class helps me avoid saying something stupid or foolish. It protects me from being put down by others. It protects me from having my mental competence judged by others."

At a deeper level, some patterns function as a protective shield against some basic self-doubt. In class, we call this basic self-doubt a "crusher." The crusher is a negative belief about oneself that highlights an inadequacy. To confront this belief directly is very frightening, so a defensive pattern is created to avoid acknowledging the fact that one believes it. When the student in our example was helped to probe a bit deeper, she identified her crusher this way: "I doubt my intellectual competency. I'm afraid I'm not as smart as others in the class. I keep thinking that my opinions are of such low calibre that others would laugh if I let them out into the open."

Consequences. The students are now asked to evaluate their pattern in terms of how effectively or efficiently it serves them and at what cost. Some patterns are more psychologically "expensive" than others. To determine such costs, students react to the following question: Suppose you could never change or alter the set of responses that make up your pattern; it would be "frozen" in its present form the remainder of your life. As a consequence of this, what opportunities or experiences might be forever denied to you?

A sample response to this question was: "Well, one way I pay for being so quiet is that I never get a chance to express myself in public. I have to stay 'private' and feel alone and isolated. My ideas and feelings don't get a chance to interact with anyone else's. I'm always holding back and that's not very satisfying. I get particularly annoyed when something I was thinking of saying is expressed by someone else and everyone thinks it's great. Meanwhile, I sit there stewing over the fact that I could have said that. I guess, too, my passivity carries over into other situations that I'm not even aware of."

Experimenting. When the student, after determining the cost of the pattern, feels that she is paying a very high price for the momentary safety it provides, she may decide to explore some improved forms of responding. However, in order to experiment fully with new or different sets of responses, the student must develop a new attitude that counteracts the power of the crusher and supplies the courage to nourish the experimental responses. Students are asked to create a belief about themselves that would contradict the crusher. Because it is so difficult to believe that contradiction, we call it a "direction," a belief to aim for, to try on over and over until it begins to sound and feel more valid. This phase of the process is usually the most emotionally intense as students struggle to bring this contradictory belief to life. A variety of self-re-enforcing strategies are suggested to the class for this purpose.

Here are some examples of crushers and their corresponding directions.

From: "If I don't continually serve the needs of others, I'm worthless." (This particular crusher seems to be very prevalent for the women in the classes.)
To: "Taking care of my own needs can really be helpful to others."
From: "I have to be very careful about what I say, or people will discover how really dumb I am."
To: "Any opinion I have is worth expressing!"
From: "I'm too incompetent to make any significant decision."
To: "I have a perfect right to make good and bad decisions!"
From: "If I don't keep myself under control at all times, I'll disintegrate."
To: "I can lose control and fully exist!"; or "Allowing myself to collapse shows I'm in control!"

Once some practice with directions is achieved, students, using some models from behavioral therapy, begin to design experiments for trial outside of class. They construct a hierarchical set of experiments from the least fearful to the most fearful and contract with their support groups which ones they will try during the following week.

Evaluation. How did the experiment work? What happened as a consequence? What needs to be changed, if anything, in the design? Does it need to be repeated in some other situations?

The responses to these and other questions are reported to the support group after each experiment. Plans and new contracts are then developed for continuing trials.

Choice. As a result of this procedure, it is hoped that the student has more choices available with which to respond to certain situations; that is, they have expanded their repetoire for responsiveness.

The entire procedure for each student is carefully documented and recorded in individual journals. These are summarized and submitted to the instructor at the end of the semester as a final paper.

Summary

A highly complex set of interactions constitutes "Education of the Self."* The course attempts to introduce into a formal educational institution those learning opportunities that are highly personal, intellectually challenging, emotionally relevant, and promoting of self-knowledge. These are the basic ingredients of self-science education.

*A trainer's manual entitled *Education of the Self,* by Gerald Weinstein, Joy Hardin, and Matt Weinstein, was published in 1976 by Mandala Press of Amherst, Massachusetts. It is now out of print. However, libraries have copies. Some copies may be obtained by writing to the author of this chapter.

Gerald Weinstein is the developer of the self-science education course described in this chapter. He is a professor of education at the University of Massachusetts and has been director of the Center for Humanistic Education there. He is the coauthor and editor of Toward Humanistic Education: A Curriculum of Affect, *and author of numerous articles.*

*College, not life, is divided into courses. The
I-Division program helped students apply classroom
learning to current life programs.*

The Individual in Society: An Interdisciplinary Studies Program

Norma Watkins

All students at Miami-Dade Community College are required to enroll in several general education courses. The goal of these courses is to "provide students with the opportunity to acquire the knowledge, skills, and attitudes that are fundamental to every individual's effort to have a more satisfying life, and to function as a more effective citizen" (Miami-Dade college catalogue). Although the courses are derived from the theoretical disciplines, social science, natural science, communication, and humanities, the intent behind the requirements is clearly in the realm of application. Students are expected to acquire knowledge and skills that will help them to live more satisfying lives. The "I Curriculum" was developed by faculty in the Division of Intercurricular Studies at Miami-Dade. The curriculum provided an interdisciplinary, experiential approach to the general education requirements, combining affective and cognitive approaches to education. Students learned about the world at the same time that they were learning about themselves. Because the program was concerned with applications of knowledge in everyday life, traditional teaching techniques were widely supplemented with field work and other experiences in which students actively engaged new ideas, new skills, and new attitudes toward present and future life issues. The various disciplines were treated as separate courses but as different and interrelated approaches to problems.

Curriculum

The two-semester curriculum focused on "man as an individual" and "man in society." Part One, "Man (or woman) as an individual" addressed itself to the following question: "How can each of us be the person she or he would like to be?" Each student answered by examining facts and theories from the fields of natural science, social science, sociology, psychology, and communications. The students assessed their initial skills and attitudes toward themselves. They mapped out their current behavior patterns, their personal development, and the limits on their lives, such as aging, poor health, lack of financial resources, and so on. To culminate the semester's work, students drew up a life plan in which they contrasted their current life style to their ideal life style. They assessed the changes they had to make to achieve their personal goals and began to plan a life strategy for moving in the desired directions.

Part Two, "Man in Society," focused on the students' interaction with their natural and social environments. It addressed itself to the question: "How can each of us more effectively interact with and control the forces in our natural and social environment?" The students answered by examining facts and theories from the fields of natural science, social science, sociology, and communications. They began by identifying and examining current U.S. problems, constraints encountered in nature and society, and the global framework of many problems facing humanity. To culminate their term's work, the students engaged in a project that integrated the knowledge they had gained by planning a solution to a social or environmental problem, and by testing and evaluating their proposed solutions.

Grades and a fair system for rewarding students for different levels of cognitive and affective achievement were also components of the program. Finally, the interdisciplinary program had to be cost effective. All faculty members who were involved had to teach the same number of students for which they were generally responsible at no additional cost to the college.

Program Outline

A typical, two-semester student program comprised the following: *First semester:* English, Social Science, Interdisciplinary Science, Human Relations; *Second semester:* English, Social Science, Interdisciplinary Science, Social Problems.

The first semester focused on the individual, on the assumption that students could not know the world until they had an authentic picture of themselves. They could not empathize with others until they had affirmed themselves. This was a logical though somewhat artificial distinction between inner and outer realities. The first semester of social science contained equal portions of anthropology, sociology, and psychology. Students were asked to define themselves in a cultural context by examining norms, values, and beliefs of the people in their cultural milieu. They looked at their own sense of class, status, and role-related behavior. In studying the concept of ethnocentrism, they examined their own stereotypes, prejudices, symbol systems, and overall world view. Students applied theories of socialization to themselves by comparing concepts of the "looking glass self" (Coley, 1909), cultural pressure, and behavioral reinforcement. In the English course, students assessed their current skills in reading and writing. They examined their own patterns of oral communication and symbolic interaction. They learned and applied theories of nonverbal communication and examined the impact of their own language on their thoughts and beliefs. In Human Relations, students examined their definitions of self-concept and the ways they functioned intellectually, spiritually, and emotionally. They examined the capacity they had for growth in these areas and the limits on such growth. In Natural Science, students examined the relationship between habits and health by assessing their own health habits: eating, sleeping, drinking, drugs, exercise. They learned the roles of the biological systems affecting cycles of growth, maturation, and aging. They looked at genetics as a basis for human problems, and at basic physiological needs and the possibility of ideal health.

All the activities and topics described were organized to help students achieve the five learning goals for the semester: (1) Determining where you are, (2) Understanding how you function, (3) Determining how you became the person you are, (4) Coming to grips with the limits of human behavior, (5) Becoming the person you want to be. The approaches to all the goals were experiential and interdisciplinary. Goal Five provided the opportunity for students to synthesize their learning from the first four goals. A somewhat detailed description of the activities related to Goal Five follows.

Becoming the Person You Want To Be

Just as the discipline content within each goal area is ultimately integrated into one or more total evaluations by the student, the four goals themselves are finally integrated into an ultimate student evaluation. Having a working knowledge of where they are, how they function, what determined their individualities, and what ultimate limits of life they must face, the students are prepared to integrate this knowledge in the synthesis of a life plan. At this point in the curriculum, cognitive and affective objectives merge as the students, armed with a comprehensive body of cognitive knowledge, are in a position to make some far-reaching decisions about their futures. The ability to determine their futures, using carefully-laid foundations of sound cognitive material, is the ultimate process of a meaningful education. The I-Division course work is designed to culminate in the highest possible educational goal—the intelligent self-determination by the student. With the cognitive tools of a knowledge of the elements of current lifestyle, ideal lifestyles, and possibilities of change, the student can formulate a logical, intelligent life plan (Watkins, 1975, p. 67).

With this introduction, students were instructed to integrate what they had learned in their courses in English, psychology, interdisciplinary science, and social science by formulating a statement that described their current lifestyles, their ideal lifestyles, and a plan for the changes to be made if they were to move from current situations to ideal ones. The instructors provided a series of worksheets and projects to assist students in formulating the plan.

Sample Questions and Activities

Questions on Current Lifestyles included: (1) Describe how you see yourself and how you think others see you; (2) Describe your ability to communicate in written and oral form; (3) Describe where you live; (4) Describe your material possessions; (5) Describe your eating habits, where, when, what, and how much you eat; (6) Describe your physical health; (7) Describe the meaning of your life right now.

Questions on ideal lifestyles included: (1) What are the highest values in your life right now? (2) If you could make your life more ideal in any way, how would you change? (3) Answer the questions about your current lifestyle in terms of your ideal. Be practical. Take into account the probable as well as the possible.

Questions on changing current lifestyles included: (1) In moving from your present lifestyle to your ideal, what pitfalls must you avoid? What weaknesses must you overcome? (2) Identify your strengths; (3) Identify your value conflicts; (4) List the changes that you can begin to make now, in six months, in one year; (5) As you begin to make these changes, where will you begin? How will you decide what changes should be made first? (6) Picture yourself living your ideal life. Describe a typical day in your life, as if you were living it now.

The final product was a poster-sized road map, tracing each student's path from their present self to their ideal self, with all the goals, strengths, skills, obstacles, weaknesses, and time dimensions colored in.

Being in the World

In the second semester, the vision turned outward: in the social sciences, toward economics and political science; in Englsh, toward research methods; in the sciences, toward the environment; and in Social Problems, toward the human community.

Whenever possible, the activities were interdisciplinary, satisfying learning objectives from several disciplines simultaneously. One such activity was a Body Fair. The fair itself, where students were weighed, measured, tested for body type, lung capacity, blood type and, certain genetic characteristics satisfied a science objective. By investigating their feelings about their health and taking responsibility for it, students satisfied a human relations objective. By examining the facets of their health that might be culturally influenced, they satisfied a social science objective. By writing about the experience and keeping a log of sleeping and eating habits, they satisfied a communications objective.

Student Evaluation

The student evaluation systems was oriented around Bloom's Taxonomy (Bloom, 1956). Course objectives satisfied the various levels of learning described by Bloom.

Grade Level	Learning Level	Definition and Example
D	Knowledge and Comprehension	Remembering and understanding an idea or fact in a form close to the way it was presented.
C	Application	Implies comprehension; applying a fact to a real or simulated situation; for example, defining "value" and identifying three personal values.
B	Analysis and Synthesis	Analysis involves the breakdown of the material into its parts and perceiving the relationship between the parts. Synthesis is defined as putting the parts together to form a whole, combining information into patterns and structures.
A	Evaluation	Making judgments about the value of ideas, methods or materials; Involves some combination of all other behaviors—knowledge, comprehension, application, analysis, synthesis.

The grading code identified a learning objective with a course, a goal, and a level of difficulty. For example, "SSS328" referred to a social science objective found in Goal Three, learning level two (Grade C), objective eight in Goal Three. Students completed as many objectives under each goal as they wished to complete, potentially working their way up to an A in each course. Using a computer program developed for this course, students were able to assess their current level of accomplishment and potential grade at any point in the semester.

Structure and Interpersonal Needs

The success of the I-Division curriculum depended not so much on the design of the course as on the willingness of the team of teachers to work together, to understand each other's disciplines, and to believe in interdisciplinary, experiential learning. The five-person team consisted of an English professor, a social scientist, a natural scientist, a psychologist, and a coordinator who was also based in the English department. Each instructor was responsible for about thirty-five students. The class met in a circular room divided like pie wedges into small meeting areas, with the center as an open core. The structure of the meeting room reflected the structure of the learning activities. All 200 students could meet in the same time and space. The smaller class "families" met in the sub-units. Lectures and large group activities like the Body Fair involved the total group. The subgroups worked together throughout the semester, accomplishing as many objectives as possible in each group, including all the affective objectives. The model satisfied the not-so-obvious needs of students in a commuter college. The I-Division model provided a home base for students as they progressed through their required courses. In addition to completing the general education requirements, the students had an opportunity to overcome their isolation in the new environment of the community college. The coordination among the various instructors and the high level of interaction among the students satisfied educational and interpersonal requirements simultaneously.

Program Values

In their approach to teaching, the faculty modeled their belief in interdisciplinary, experiential learning. Since college is divided into courses, but life is not, classroom activities demonstrated the integration and integrity of learning. Students saw that each learning experience contained elements of communication, societal influence, awareness of the biological self, and understanding of human relationships. They learned how knowledge and skills acquired in class could enable them to "live a more satisfying life and function as a more effective citizen" (Miami-Dade college catalogue). Because of this integration between living and learning, achieving academic objectives became a challenge instead of a chore.

References

Bloom, B. *Taxonomy of Educational Objectives.* New York: Longman, Green, 1956.
Coley, C. *Social Organization.* New York: Scribner's, 1909.
Watkins, N. *Student Handbook.* Miami, Fla.: South Campus, Miami-Dade Community College, 1975.

Norma Watkins is on the faculty of Miami-Dade Community College and was coordinator of the program described in this chapter. She earned her Ph.D. degree through the Union Graduate School.

Student development staff and academic faculty must develop a common language and mutual respect if they are to function together effectively.

Facts, Feelings, and Academic Credit

Margaret Barr
Jane Fried

"Facts are the enemy of Truth"—Don Quixote.
"Whether the stone hits the pitcher or the pitcher hits the stone, it's going to be bad for the pitcher"
                                        Sancho Panza

Faculty members and student affairs staffs seem to be on campus for vastly different purposes and typically have very different points of view about any campus phenomenon. The presence and value of faculty members antedates the presence of acknowledged value of student-affairs staffs. Chief administrative officers on many campuses tend to see the major role of student-affairs staffs as keeping the students under control so that they will not embarrass the administration. Prior (1973) and Bloland (1979) assert that there is no widespread interest in the developmental function in which student affairs professes to be expert. Bloland contends that the market for work in student affairs on campus is still in the realm of student service, management, and control.

Faculty functions, however, are seen as basic to the existence of any college: the creation, transmission, and application of knowledge. Most entering freshmen see academic, not personal, concerns as absolutely primary (Sagaria and others, 1980). Students who have adequate and satisfying interaction with faculty during their own college careers tend to express more satisfaction with all other dimensions of their college experience (Astin, 1977).

The purpose of this chapter is to sketch the broad dimensions of the difference between the "typical" faculty mind set about the purposes of higher education and the "typical" mind set of the student-affairs staff about the same phenomenon. In many ways, faculty and student-affairs administrators constitute two distinct subcultures on many campuses. They have different values, attitudes, and languages. Even in areas where there is a strong tradition of humanism, in colleges whose goal is to educate the "whole student," student-affairs staff and academic faculty typically go about their educational business in drastically different fashions, generally in totally different locations on campus. As student-development education moves toward the classroom, student-development educators must become "bicultural," learning the norms and language of the faculty in order to make better communication possible. Appropriate metaphors for this process include "translation" as well as ' acculturation." In an effort to help student-development education become an important focus for any campus (Crookston, 1973; King and Fields, 1980), student-development staff must learn to speak the language of those in whose country they are beginning to travel.

Essential Contrasts

Faculty are ostensibly in the business of pursuing truth wherever they find it—in the laboratory, the library, or the labyrinth of the human mind. Their job is to discover Truth and examine facts in its light. Finally, they create a vision of what is true, illustrate it with facts, and teach it to students. For engaging in this business, faculty are rewarded with promotion, tenure, academic freedom, a faculty senate, and whatever equipment is necessary and affordable for the furtherance of this pursuit. In the minds of many academicians, the faculty is the college. This has been true since the Middle Ages. This state of affairs confers enormous power on the faculty as well as a sense of essential "rightness" about the way things are.

Student-affairs staff have a lot in common with Sancho Panza, who focuses for the most part on the practical side of life, leaving others to pursue the transcendent values of beauty, truth, chastity, and valor. By the nature of their role in the campus community, student-affairs staff attend to the less predictable aspects of campus life.

Faculty tend to see students under orderly circumstances—in the classroom, the laboratory, and appointed advising sessions. Under these circumstances, students usually arrive punctually, attempt to complete assigned or chosen tasks, take exams, solve problems, and demonstrate that they have learned in a prescribed time, place, and manner.

In contrast, student-affairs staff see students in less structured circumstances, such as residence halls, counseling interactions, social events, placement activities, and organizational meetings. Time demands for these activities are usually less rigid, and students engage in them based on their own needs and desires. Learning often comes through trial and error, with resultant pain, disappointment, and frustrations. The world of the student-affairs staff is not orderly; in fact, it is filled with emotions, crises, and the pain of maturation. Despite the best-laid plans, the unexpected is frequently the order of the day.

This contrast does not imply that faculty do not have to deal with disorder in their world. Anyone familiar with academic administration knows that this is not true. However, in their main function of teaching and research, the faculty do inhabit a more predictable environment than the student-affairs staff.

Given the different worlds or environments that faculty and student-affairs staff inhabit, differences emerge with regard to assumptions about the learning process, work behaviors, and standards of professional behavior. By the nature of their primary work, the faculty lives in a professional world of abstraction, where numerous ideas are discussed and the right to examine any point of view is guaranteed by the principle of academic freedom. The processes of curriculum development and theory building are generally more logical than experiential. Trained in deductive reasoning, the academician moves intellectually from the accepted principles of a discipline to their logical extensions. There is rarely any demand to apply a new theory to a campus problem in attempting to develop an immediate solution. Scientific research is done in several stages. Basic research is conducted in laboratories, under conditions that are as controlled as possible. If a logically constructed principle and its tested application turn out to be in error, the principle is reexamined or a new experiment is designed. There is no immediate impact on public policy or public behavior. Research applications in which the public is involved occur much later in the process. In research involving human subjects, the conditions of application are stringently controlled to avoid danger to humans. The faculty is buffered from exposing its work in the political arena until the concepts and applications have been tested and examined repeatedly.

Student-affairs administrators have no such buffer. Trained in the basics of administrative and counseling theory, they are forced into working in the "self-as-instrument" mode (Combs, 1949), especially when responding to crises. Instantaneous response is often required in many situations, with no prolonged period for thought or reflection permitted within the constraints of the particular problem. When a student or a student group asks for help, the first response is based on a combination of the administrator's personality and training (Combs, 1969). The principles that govern that person's behavior have become internalized. These principles may be based in theory, but they are frequently understood only as hunches about what would be best in the situation. Logic follows, if there is a moment for contemplation after the dust settles. Thinking is often inductive: "After working with so many students for so much time, what have I learned? What *works* with students? What doesn't work? When should I be firm? Flexible?"

Within the last decade, many divisions of student affairs have been conducting research, particularly in the area of environmental assessment. Such research efforts provide a stronger data base for problem solving and crisis intervention. In addition, such research efforts assist the student-affairs staff in anticipating problems and logically developing a proposed course of action. Such approaches should be encouraged; however, too few institutions have developed such intensive research programs. Student-affairs professionals often lack training for clear-headed debate over ideas and their implications. Since the ultimate criteria for judging the value of an idea within student affairs are often based in the individual's experience, there are few accepted principles of evaluation against which principles and practices of student affairs can be judged. In a discussion of how to approach a problem, individuals often conflict over the relative weight of their own experiential learning and the relative truth of what each has learned. Since learning is frequently based on personal experience, disputes over ideas and approaches can easily deteriorate into personal battles. Since principles of professional effectiveness are often derived idiosyncratically, without reference to a large body of accepted theory, it is extremely difficult for one person to challenge another's conclusions on grounds of generally accepted principles. There are simply very few generally accepted principles.

From this set of contrasts, it is apparent that faculty and student-affairs administrators function in very different worlds on campus. Each group interprets differently the data of campus events and generates proper solutions to campus problems. Each group also views the learning process from a different perspective.

Contrasting Work Environments

In the daily world of campus activity, student-affairs administrators and academic faculty generally work under very different circumstances. Faculty teach, conduct research, and revise course content as necessary. The rate of change in the academic universe is relatively slow. Faculty control over graduation requirements is firm. Once a student enters the university in a particular program, the student will generally follow the rules established therein. Faculty, knowing the number of majors in a discipline, can reasonably predict how many sections of each course will be required and plan months in advance about the distribution of teaching assignments. Many faculty have tenure and are hired in particular academic specialties. Teaching in a new academic area, for which current faculty are not trained, generally requires the hiring of a new member who is appropriately trained.

Faculty are clearly considered experts in their chosen fields. Course content, sequence of courses, and control over the contexts in which students apply what they have learned are also the province of the faculty. A professor of literature will not tell a professor of physics what to include in a course in fluid dynamics, nor will the physicist be consulted about the content of a course in modern American poetry. Faculty are generally expected to teach what they have learned to students who do not yet know the course content. Students are generally not expected to learn what is not known by the faculty or to discover new knowledge. The parameters of significant knowledge in any field are determined by the faculty. The faculty divides all knowledge into appropriate segments, called specialties, and further into courses, and then they teach it to the students. Students are expected to learn both content and analytic processes and demonstrate what they have learned to the faculty. Students learn the information and the research methods and then demonstrate mastery. The focus of faculty-student interaction is primarily on knowledge. The pace of student progress is expected to be fairly similar among students. Some students have to study harder to master the information at the required rate, but all students presumably should know the minimum amount of information necessary to pass a course by the end of the semester.

Student-development educators, who are in general student-affairs administrators, view the learning process differently from most academic faculty. Even in a student-development class, when topics and themes are considered in a standard sequence, there are few right answers and less external information to be mastered. Rather than focusing on information mastery, student-development courses tend to integrate information with personal meaning. For example, a developmental course in "Life Transitions" would presumably include information about the various types of life transitions; but it would also require that the faculty member be willing to share some personal experiences on the topic and that the students would be expected to discuss their own experiences and speak with members of their own family or others about transitions in their own lives.

Outside the classroom, student-development educators see learning occur daily, but do not often think of themselves as "teachers." Various student leaders can attend skill-training workshops and be exposed to the same information and the same demonstration of processes, yet each will come away from the training having mastered only what each was ready for at that particular time. Mastery will be different for each person. "Success" will be measured by future effectiveness in leading groups, not by adherence to the tenents of the training program. Rarely would a student be required to attend a leadership-training program or be removed from office for not attending a program. Although it is known that student-development educators can help students learn new skills, it is also known that some students already have these skills and do not need additional training. Indeed, sometimes undergraduate students teach in these training programs. There is no perception of a clearly defined body of skills and information for student-development educators or a monopoly on knowledge, such as the academic faculty is presumed to have.

Contrasting Expectations for Professional Performance

Student-affairs administrators are usually expected to respond to crises immediately and to solve problems as quickly as possible. The administrative world is a world of action, consequences, and accountability. The pace of change is faster. The types of controls over student behavior are viewed as broader, somewhat more parental, and less academically legitimate. The bulk of administrative controls are considered to be less powerful than academic controls. For many, "social" or "residence hall" probation is not half as frightening as "academic" probation. The former can be viewed as a minor problem with unknown future consequences. Academic probation, in contrast, can easily lead to failing out of school, and the pathway to the door is clearly marked by declining grade-point averages. If one residence hall has a catastrophically destructive party on a Friday night, the student-affairs administration is expected by many within the community to have remedies in motion by Monday morning. Although most of the chief officers of student affairs would agree that attention should be paid to the need to strengthen the student government in the hall, at a time of crisis such discussions are usually not of prime interest. Usually they are pressured to take visible action and try to assure that such behavior will be stopped in the future. Long-term educational/preventive measures are usually encouraged only when short-term, action-oriented responses are clear and visible. Such behavior is understandable, given publicity and parental and student reactions, and they do contrast sharply with acceptable ways of dealing with problems in the academic area.

If the students' grades begin to decline in a course, or if "grade inflation" hits the campus, the trend is studied before an appropriate response can be determined. This process can extend over an entire academic year. If grades begin to decline, student preparation and motivation are often first assumed to be the initial cause of the problem. A review of the appropriateness of teaching methods to the student population is often only viewed as a contributing factor when the initial thesis is proven to be unsound.

If, after careful study, a contributing cause of declining grades is found to be the academic preparation of students, then two solutions are usually proposed by the faculty. A recommendation can be made to raise admissions standards, or a proposal for a remedial course can be made. If the alternative is a remedial course, then additional time will be needed.

Student-affairs administrators have contributed to this slowness of change in the academic community by continually expressing concern that changes in requirements be instituted in a manner that does not penalize currently enrolled students.

Given these circumstances, the insertion of a remedial course into a degree program will take up to two years. Approvals must be gained by committees and governing bodies, all of which require extensive debate on the issues. Faculty are often working to implement solutions to a problem recognized as long as two years before. Monday-morning solutions to such academic concerns are rarely required.

These contrasts in expectations of action are brought into focus in the development of courses for academic credit that deal with the broad area of student development. The processes of decision making within the academic context must be accounted for in any proposal that is instructional in nature. Legitimization of developmental instruction requires academic involvement on the part of the student-affairs staff, as instructors and instructional consultants. Bridges must therefore be built between student-affairs administrators, who are the specialists in student-development education, and academicians, who are the content specialists and instructional faculty. Translation must occur when academicians and student-development educators speak to each other, if the two groups want to make the intellectual connections that will expand student-development education into classroom settings. Since many academicians do not feel the need to discuss student development with student-affairs staff, and feel less of a need to welcome student-affairs people as consultants into either the faculty or their own classrooms, it behooves the people in student affairs to begin building the bridges and doing the translation. In this fashion, a transformation process can begin in which students can learn "the processes of discovering what is known and applying that knowledge to a deeper understanding of self, of enhancing the quality of relationships with others, and of coping effectively with their world" (Crookston, 1973, p. 52). This new teaching/learning model transcends the traditional concepts of academic disciplines, breaks down the split between learning in class and learning out of class, and overcomes the great divide between knowledge of theory and ability to apply theory to practice in many dimensions of life. It also generates resistance from people on both sides of the fence.

Translation

Faculty and student-affairs administrators often speak two different languages. The former deal in logic and theory, providing a map for understanding large areas of human knowledge and experience. The latter most often speak a language of empiricism, intuition, and application, focusing their problem-solving abilities on problems unique to the particular time and space they occupy. When student-affairs administrators begin to move toward the world of credit-bearing courses, they must translate their own goals, values, programs, and resources into a language that curriculum committees can understand and deans appreciate.

Course proposals must be built step by step in the format outlined by the curriculum committee or academic department that will review the proposal. The theoretical basis of the course must be clearly described. If the course is to be interdisciplinary (which most student-development courses are), then all disciplines must be acknowledged, but the discipline of the sponsoring department must be primary. A topical outline of the subject to be covered is critical, and that outline must flow from one topic to another in a disciplinary perspective. Student-development educators tend to think in terms of sequences and skill training and often leave the reasons for a particular sequence or organizational unit unstated. In speaking with academicians, the reasons for a sequence of topics and a discussion of theories that govern the presentation are generally more important than any methodology used or any skills that students will learn. The focus must be on content when course proposals are presented to academic departments. Proposing the same program to a student-affairs staff would usually shift the focus to process.

Translation is a powerful function. When student-development educators move into the academic arena, they are often "Strangers in a Strange Land" (Heinlein, 1968) and must negotiate in the language of the majority group. There is a vast potential for misunderstanding or making assumptions about what individuals from the other group mean, think, and can or cannot do. Academicians are specialists at defining terminology. Accuracy in defining terminology is a major aspect of the ability of faculty to collaborate with colleagues and conceptualize and investigate academic problems. Student-development educators are specialists at helping others to clarify their personal meanings and values and at restating meanings in terms that both parties can understand. Such skills are critical to the effectiveness of any student-development educator or counselor and are very important to employ in any discussion of course proposals in student development. A well-managed discussion will enable the student-development educator to present a clear proposal in academically sound terms, answer questions with a clear understanding of the questioner's agenda, and improve communication in general between members of that academic committee and educators in student development. A poorly managed discussion can lead to hostility, misunderstanding, and an increase in mistrust between faculty and student-development staff. The key to a good discussion in this context is to be sure that all important terms are understood in the same context by all persons involved.

Bridges and Networks

As in any human organization, who you know in academia is as important as what you know. Presenting a proposal to a curriculum committee for a course in student development is the capstone in a series of collaborative relationships that develop over a long period of time. The relationship may be difficult if the interaction between members of the student-affairs division and the faculty is limited to times when student affairs is trying to acquire some faculty prerogative. Even in areas where support for student-development education is strong, faculty are often reluctant to share the classroom with members of the student-affairs staff (Heavilin, 1980).

Bridges of respect and networks of understanding between the subcultures of faculty and student affairs can be built in a variety of ways. People in higher education often see themselves as overworked and faced with a variety of frustrating but unavoidable problems. Simpson's case study is a good example of such a situation, as is the study by Parker and Kreps (see earlier chapters in this sourcebook). Any course that is causing difficulty because students cannot succeed in it is usually a good location for an offer of assistance by student-development staff who can teach study skills, test-taking strategies, or any other type of academic support skill. Classes that are discussion oriented can generally benefit from alternative teaching approaches like role playing or other types of structured exercises. Teaching assistants may be more open than others to offers of assistance in helping to generate a more lively classroom atmosphere.

Career-development officers have collaborated effectively with faculty in helping students develop career plans that are relevant to their major. A successful example of this cooperative approach has been instituted by the Career Planning and Placement Office at Northern Illinois University. Assisting a college of liberal arts in designing career-planning courses for liberal arts majors can help maintain enrollments in the liberal arts during a time of enrollment declines.

Residence halls also provide ideal locations for expanding the types of contact between faculty, students, and student-affairs staff. Options can range from an invitation to dinner to a discussion session to a special interest academic floor. There are numerous ways for faculty and student-development staff to collaborate in creating effective residence hall programs and provide enriched learning opportunities for students. The key to success of this type of effort is the notion of "collaboration between colleagues." For collaboration to be effective and to lead to improvements in student life, faculty members and student-development staff must work together, think together, and benefit from their joint effort. In this process, mutual respect and understanding improve and grow between faculty and student-affairs staff.

On-Campus Research Projects

Faculty can also be effectively involved in applying their research skills to difficult campus problems like vandalism. For example, the Task Force on Vandalism at the University of Connecticut was composed of student-affairs staff, police, clergy, students, and faculty from the sociology, psychology, and environmental design departments. The task force yielded: (1) a broad description of the problem of vandalism on campus, (2) several research projects that provided either dissertation material or publishable information, (3) systematic efforts to improve the physical environment in several pilot residence halls, (4) employment for one graduate research assistant, (5) numerous educational programs, (6) improved efforts to support "responsible drinking" and minimize drunkenness, (7) an accurate data-gathering system for accumulating information about campus vandalism in the future, and (8) revisions in the disciplinary procedures.

More than twenty people who do not ordinarily work together collaborated on finding solutions to a problem that affected all of them in one way or another. As a result, each subgroup gained an increased understanding of the problems that the others faced in their work at the university and the skills and knowledge that each brings to bear in coping with these problems. All groups received some tangible benefit and the turf was neutral.

Membership on Faculty Committees

Student-affairs staff can identify many ways to invite faculty into their domain and involve them in helping to solve problems or examine issues that affect students in and out of class. Staff members in student affairs should also involve themselves in solving campus-wide problems or joining campus-wide committees that are typically under the control of the faculty. Most faculty senates have student-life committees and other subcommittees to which student-development staff can contribute their time and knowledge. Even if membership is not open, meetings often are. Remember that knowledge is power! Student-affairs staff have knowledge of certain dimensions of campus life of which faculty are unaware and have skills that faculty often lack. By becoming involved in activities that are typically faculty dominated, student-development staff will be better known by faculty who might not otherwise realize that they exist, and will gain credibility by contributing time, knowledge, and skill to the solution of particular problems. They will also begin to gain some insight into the power politics of the faculty, their jargon, their values, and their particular points of view. Although student-affairs people feel themselves to be as overworked as anybody else, this process of self-involvement with faculty committees cannot be viewed simply as more work. It is part of the professional education of people who are moving toward faculty responsibility in the field of student-development education. It is an acculturation into a new dimension of the university community and provides a critical base for future interactions.

Implementation of Courses in Student Development

The planning phases for the creation and implementation of courses in student development are not radically different from planning and implementing any other educational program. Two skills are critical to this process: the ability to translate the goals and purposes of the proposed course and the interaction skills and credibility of the proposer. The persons who lead the efforts for these courses must consider themselves as colleagues of the faculty. The individual proposer needs to have the academic credentials required by the department to which the course is being proposed. If the course proposal is successful, student-affairs teachers may need to hold adjunct faculty status. Thus, their credentials must be equivalent to other faculty, even though transfer of fiscal resources and the question of tenure are not at issue.

The following steps provide a useful guide to student-affairs staff in developing sound course proposals. Each step has merit, but the process of implementation may vary from campus to campus.

Document the Need for and Desirability of the Proposed Course

Most courses in student-development can be justified from the side of student affairs as efforts at preventative mental health or outreach counseling. From the faculty side, the course must be justified in terms of its relevance to the discipline of the department and its curricular orientation; for example, a course in peer counseling was justified to a Department of Educational Psychology because it paralleled in many ways a graduate introductory course in counseling methods and could be seen as a "feeder" into that graduate program. Additional information regarding the desirability of the proposed course should be presented in terms of departmental priorities and concerns (for example, increased departmental enrollment figures at no increased cost; increased departmental ability to meet the needs of a particular subpopulation).

At this stage, it is important to obtain some support from a full-time member of the sponsoring department. Such a colleague can give guidance on the issue of departmental priorities and explain the informal power structure of departmental decision making. The colleague can also alert the presenter to topics that are "red flags" to the department, issues to avoid, if possible, and language to use in making any presentation. If the student-development person must be a translator, the faculty colleague can be seen as the informal protocol officer for the other side. If the department or school has a written guide for the form in which such proposals must be submitted, follow the guide scrupulously.

Organize Available Resources

Once again, this is relatively simple to do on the student-affairs side. If the course will be taught by teams, or involve guest lecturers, identify these resources within the student-affairs division. Do a check of library materials that cover the subject. Include in the resource bank the faculty members from the academic department who are supportive of the proposal. Test the components of the process against their challenges. Encourage faculty colleagues to dissect the proposal so that it can be rearranged in terms that are comprehensible to both student-development staff and the academic department. Respond to their challenges and solicit their criticism. Create, if possible, a proposal that faculty members can support in a departmental meeting with their faculty colleagues. By making every effort to understand and appreciate their criticisms and concerns, you can answer their challenges prior to any formal hearing on a proposal, and fewer challenges will result when the formal action is taken.

Plan the Course and Write the Proposal

In format, follow the standard form for course proposals. Indicate goals for the course, sequences of content areas or topics, and procedures for evaluating student performance and the course itself. A good guideline is to focus heavily on the content to be covered, not the teaching methods to be used. Attach a brief bibliography and suggest a range of textbooks. One strategy is to minimize or omit any goals related purely to personal growth or other affective areas. Instead, focus on course objectives that can be described in terms of skill or information mastery and be evaluated accordingly. Affective development is typically not of concern to academic departments. Usually their position is neutral, but, at worst, any mention of personal growth goals in an academic course proposal can yield an accusation that psychotherapy will occur in class. This accusation will generally lead to the defeat of the proposal.

The proposal will probably appear dull to the author and will probably not convey the exciting essence of what is supposed to happen in the course. What is exciting to student-development staff is not necessarily exciting to academic faculty. They are looking for logic, order, a solid research base, and a certain amount of academically sound information. In proposing a course through an academic department, you are asking that department to take overall responsibility for an activity of the student-affairs staff. If they are taking responsibility, they deserve to have their standards for legitimacy satisfied. None of them wants to be subject to the criticism of having offered courses without academic substance under departmental sponsorship.

Present the Proposal to the Department or Curriculum Committee

Conform to the standard schedule for new course proposals. The requests may be considered as early as ten months before any new course is implemented. It is not unusual for departments to meet only once a month and for requests to appear on the agenda two weeks before the meeting. Honor the timetable and whatever other protocol is involved. Do not cause an emergency. It is usually helpful to provide multiple copies of any proposal and give the committee time to read it again prior to discussion, and then to provide a verbal summary to begin the discussion. During the discussion, keep in mind a clear sense of departmental and academic values. Remember that your purpose is to understand their point of view and to answer questions in terms that make sense to them. If terminology is confusing, ask for clarification. If the issue of awarding academic credit comes up, ask what criteria are typically employed in determining credit-worthiness for other courses in their department or discipline. These comments usually take the form, "This is all very interesting and useful, but why should we give students credit for learning it? I learned about X on my own time, not in a classroom." Answer the question in the terms that the questioner defines. Do not assume that the faculty share student-development values, priorities, or knowledge. You are an outsider. You have to translate. You have to speak as carefully in this setting as you would speak to a gendarme in Paris after only two years of high school French. Remember you do not want to be misunderstood and it is not your native language.

It is extremely important that the presenter of the proposal maintain composure during the discussion. Academicians are experienced in heated debates and pride themselves on their ability to separate personal feelings from conflicts over ideas. Student-affairs people do not typically separate conflict over ideas from conflict between persons. It is therefore very easy to become defensive when ideas are challenged in this context. Be aware of the dynamics of the group during the discussion. Be sensitive to the support you are receiving from your well-informed allies and, if necessary, follow their lead for appropriate behavior in the group.

Be clear about the parts of your proposal that can be compromised and the parts that are crucial to the integrity of the course. Be ready to compromise as desirable. Willingness to compromise includes compromising both course content and procedural details. To illustrate, if you are expected to be assigned a permanent course number and they assign you an experimental number (that is, a course that is subject to review every semester for a limited number of semesters), take the experimental number. Use the alloted time to build up an excellent course and valid evaluation data. If you expected to be appointed to the faculty on an adjunct basis and the department wants a full-time member to be the instructor-of-record, give the request serious thought. Usually the instructor-of-record supervises and does not teach very much and takes the responsibility for insuring that departmental standards are met. If this person is impressed with the initial semester, such an instructor can be the most valuable ally during the next session with the department, when the course is evaluated.

Conduct the Course

Do as well as you possibly can. Refer to Fried's chapter in this sourcebook on "Principles of Design" for details. Provide in your planning for a comprehensive evaluation.

Submit the Final Evaluation Data to the Approving Body

Submit the data gathered in the evaluation process to the academic body that initially approved the course proposal. Include an outline of the course as it was actually taught, a list of textbooks, and other supporting material with the evaluation results. Outcomes of submitting such an evaluation will vary from no response to an evaluative discussion. Indicate how the standards set by the department were met. You may get no reaction. You may be invited to another meeting to discuss your results. Even if there is no reaction, documentation of the scope of your efforts and their effectiveness is useful. A precedent has been established by committing this information to writing. In academia, precedents carry a tremendous amount of weight. If the faculty at your institution believe that student-affairs staff do not teach, then you will have established that, in at least one case, a member of the student-affairs staff did teach the concepts as outlined, from the books identified, to a specific number of students with verifiable and justifiable results. In addition, although the course may have appeared slightly unorthodox, you will have established that it was conducted properly and competently by somebody who was an outsider to the faculty. The next time around, for the next person and the next proposal, the door will be slightly open.

Summary

Cooperative work with the academic side of the higher education enterprise is critical for the development of courses in student development. Student-affairs staff must be aware of and sensitive to the differences in approaches to problem solving between academic and student affairs. The student-affairs staff must develop the skills to translate course proposals in student development to faculty decision-making bodies. As part of this process, it is critical that support systems and networks be developed between academic and student-affairs staff. Generating course proposals that are acceptable to academic units is done by the processes inherent in academic change. However, such a process can produce the opportunity for positive learning experiences for students, student-affairs staff, and faculty members.

References

Adams, H. *The Academic Tribes.* New York: Liveright, 1976.
Astin, A. *Four Critical Years: Effects of College on Beliefs, Attitudes, and Knowledge.* San Francisco: Jossey-Bass, 1977.
Bloland, P. "Student Personnel Training for the Chief Student Affairs Officer: Essential or Unnecessary?" *NASPA Journal,* 1979, *17* (2), 57-62.
Combs, A. *Florida Studies in the Helping Professions.* University of Florida Monograph 37. Gainesville: University of Florida, 1969.
Combs, A., and Snygg, D. *Individual Behavior.* New York: Harper
Crookston, B. "Education for Human Development." In C. W. *Directions for College Counselors: A Handbook for Redesigning Professional Roles.* San Francisco: Jossey-Bass, 1973.
Heavilin, R. "The Curricular Legitimization of Student Development Theory." *Journal of College Student Personnel,* 1980, *21* (5), 407-413.
Heinlein, R. *Stranger in a Strange Land.* New York: Berkeley Medallion Books, 1968.
King, P., and Fields, A. "A Framework for Student Development: From S. D. Goals to Educational Opportunity Practice." *Journal of College Student Personnel,* 1980, *21* (6), 541-548.
Prior, J. "The Reorganization of Student Personnel Services: Facing Reality." *Journal of College Student Personnel,* 1973, *14* (3), 202-205.
Sagaria, M., Higginson, L., and White, E. "Perceived Needs of Entering Freshmen: The Primacy of Academic Issues." *Journal of College Student Personnel,* 1980, *21* (3), 243-247.

Margaret J. Barr is assistant vice-president for student affairs at Northern Illinois University. Prior to her present assignment, she served as associate dean of students at the University of Texas at Austin.

Jane Fried is the coordinator of student development, staff training, and research for the Office of Residential Life at the University of Connecticut. She is also an adjunct faculty member of the School of Education.

Developmental instruction makes a significant contribution to the improvement of teaching and learning in higher education.

Conclusions and Annotated References

Jane Fried

Developmental instruction is still a rather fuzzy concept. It is a function of the total academic community and can happen any place, at any time, with any number of participants. Roles can be reversed, with older people learning from younger ones and faculty from students. Developmental instruction is unusual in that it often involves a departure from discipline-oriented learning and moves toward interdisciplinary, multidimensional inquiry into the problems of the human community. No single segment of the educational staff has a monopoly on developmental instruction. Yet student-affairs professionals have the opportunity to lead the way with their knowledge of group dynamics, learning theory, and theories of adult and student development.

Leadership in the field of student-development education and developmental instruction is more than an effort to carve out a fiefdom for the student-affairs profession in educational institutions. The research base that student-development investigators have begun to create (Knefelkamp, Widick, and Parker, 1978; Morrill and Hurst, 1980) and the applications that have appeared in the educational arena constitute the beginnings of a new field of professional practice with legitimate roots in empirical and phenomenological research. Student-development educators, like other professionals in the behavioral sciences, are teaching on college campuses and conducting their research in laboratory and field settings. Knowledge generated from student-development research can be shared with academic colleagues for the purposes of broadening general insight into problems or applying what is known to the solution of those problems. Faculty members in a business school might do the same for members of a college administration, while their colleagues in a department of nutritional science provide a similar service for members of the food service staff. Information about student development can be used to help faculty members understand their students more completely. Simpson's chapter on instructional consultation illustrates one method of helping faculty improve their teaching by showing them the differences in the learning styles of students. As the age of the "typical" student changes, information from the research cited by Lester and Johnson on patterns of adult development can also be shared and discussed with faculty to help them adapt to the changing characteristics and needs of the new students. The volume of research currently in progress leaves little doubt that the study of student development has become an area of academic specialization that uses most of the investigative tools that are considered valid in other areas of applied behavioral science.

What makes the student-development profession different from other professions that are represented on teaching and research faculties is the content and context of its professional practice. Student-development educators are studying the characteristics of their research population in the location where most of the subjects spend most of their time—the college campus. They are also employed in that environment and are often expected to provide services to their subjects within the same environment. They are frequently expected to teach their subjects what they have learned about them in such a manner as to help the subjects, or students, benefit from the knowledge.

The integration of content and context is both an asset and a drawback for the emerging profession of student-development education. Since these educators remain on the college campus as activities advisors, residence hall advisors, placement officers, and so forth, it is difficult to change the public image that many faculty members hold of the student-affairs staff. If faculty see student-affairs people primarily as managers of facilities and student behavior, they may have difficulty understanding the educational functions involved in the field of student development and developmental instruction. Fortunately, the campus atmosphere makes it relatively easy to share the results of any kind of research through colloquia, seminars, informal conversations, or articles in the campus newspaper. The same types of formats can be used to inform the campus community about any substantial educational programming that is based on student-development theory and evaluated accordingly. Developmental courses and programs that involve collaboration between student-development staff and academic faculty provide an ideal showcase for introducing the profession of student-development education to a campus community. The content is interesting and affects all community members. The theoretical base is valid and expanding. The research methods are widely accepted by professionals in comparable fields. And the programs that are generated help to meet student and faculty needs in active, affirmative ways. As campus awareness increases, so does the likelihood that the profession of student-development education will increase in public effectiveness and respect.

When developmental instruction is defined as the teaching activity of student-development educators, its purpose and focus become clear. Developmental instruction is a general term that describes a series of teaching strategies that deal with problems of student learning and living and help students and staff develop skills and insight that can lead to overcoming the problems. Developmental teaching methods can improve student retention, improve learning-skill levels, improve the quality of the students' career decisions, and teach the students those skills that will help them in their professions, their relationships with others, and their own progress toward living a meaningful life.

The programs and processes described in this volume provide a brief overview of the types of contributions that the practice of student-development education and developmental instruction can make toward improving the quality of student life and education. The authors have described developmental instruction from several perspectives: (1) the dialogue between teacher and student in which both learn from each other, about each other, and about meaningful content; (2) the design process in which content, sequence, and teaching methods are integrated and connected to student learning styles and needs; and (3) the academic environment in which this type of instruction occurs. It is the editor's belief that developmental instruction, and the research and theoretical base on which it is built, constitutes a significant contribution to the improvement of teaching and learning in institutions of higher education. The practice of developmental instruction and the ability to consult with faculty in other disciplines who wish to teach developmentally provide clear evidence that the student-development profession has an educational purpose. Developmental instruction provides a method for student-affairs practitioners to continue to serve students in some of the more traditional ways while expanding the quality of service into a more academically credible and creditable mode. Developmental instruction provides clear evidence that the student-affairs staff is a part of the educational mission of a college or university.

Not all student-affairs professionals teach. Not all student services are educational. Some are managerial, some custodial. The operational functions of any division of student affairs must be maintained if a college is to run smoothly. However, student-affairs people, preceded by student-personnel workers, preceded by deans of men and women, have always asserted that their function was primarily educational. Education has always been defined by this many-named profession as more than teaching people information. Even that seventeenth-century Harvard president told his board of overseers that they were responsible for advancing *all* learning, divine and humane. Student-development education carries on in a tradition of wholistic learning. Developmental instruction provides the most effective set of modalities for student-affairs staff to live up to their historic sense of educational mission and purpose.

Annotated References

Adams, H. *The Academic Tribes.* New York: Liveright, 1976.
   A pseudo-anthropological description of the mores and politics of an academic community from a professorial point of view. Adams spent some time as an administrator, much time as an English professor. The humorous approach provokes insights that a more traditional description of academic politics might miss.
Chickering, A. *Education and Identity.* San Francisco: Jossey-Bass, 1969.
   Describes the major developmental issues that college students (ages eighteen to twenty-four) face. Provides much content for any developmental course.
Cohen, M., and March, J. *Leadership and Ambiguity.* New York: McGraw-Hill, 1969.
   A description of the decision-making processes within academic institutions. Contributes the term "organized anarchy" to the literature.
Crookston, B. "Education for Human Development." In C. Warnath (Ed.), *New Directions for College Counselors: A Handbook for Redesigning Professional Roles.* San Francisco: Jossey-Bass, 1973.
   A brief history of the general education movement, a description of "education for human/student development," and a strong argument for the centrality of student-development education in the practice of student-personnel work.
Drum, D., and Knott, G. *Structured Groups for Facilitating Development.* New York: Human Sciences Press, 1977.
   Overview of a growing mental health intervention methodology. Principles of design and programmatic examples are included.
Ivy, A., and Alschuler, A. "Psychological Education: A Prime Function of the Counselor." *The Personnel and Guidance Journal.* 1973, *51* (9).
   Psychological education parallels developmental instruction in many ways. This edition of the *P&GJ* describes two conceptual models on which psychological education can be based, various teaching techniques, and social applications for this type of education.

Knefelkamp, L., Widick, C., and Parker, C. (Eds.). *New Directions for Student Services: Applying New Developmental Findings,* no 4. San Francisco: Jossey-Bass, 1978.
  Summaries of the major theories of human development that are utilized in developmental instruction and student-development education.
Milton, O. *On College Teaching: A Guide to Contemporary Practices.* San Francisco: Jossey-Bass, 1978.
  A thorough survey of the most broadly used teaching methods on college campuses, including lecturing, discussion leading, test construction, setting of learning objectives, creating learning contracts, using simulation games, field studies, and case studies.
Morrill, W., and Hurst, J. (Eds.). *Dimensions of Interventions for Student Development.* New York: Wiley, 1980.
  An exhaustive study of student development. Presents an inclusive model of individual development, a description of environmental assessment techniques, and procedures for designing intervention strategies and evaluating effectiveness. Developmental programs in numerous campus settings are discussed and evaluated.
Parker, C. (Ed.). *Encouraging Development in College Students.* Minneapolis: University of Minnesota Press, 1978.
  Papers from a symposium that discuss student-development education as part of the curriculum and out-of-class program.
Perry, W. *Forms of Intellectual and Ethical Development in the College Years.* New York: Holt, Rinehart and Winston, 1968.
  The original presentation of the Perry theory referred to throughout this volume. Describes how students learn to think about knowledge and commitment.
Pfeiffer, J., Heslin, R., and Jones, J. *Instrumentation in Human Relations Training.* San Diego, Calif.: University Associates, 1976.
  A compendium of instruments that measure various dimensions of affective development, interpersonal skills, value formation, and self-awareness. The source for many of the tests used in Project Synergy. The tests are at various stages of validation.
Popham, J., and Sirotnik, K. *Educational Statistics, Use and Interpretation.* New York: Harper & Row, 1967.
  A useful, straightforward approach to learning statistical methods for analyzing data. Descriptions of statistical procedures are divided into two chapters each. The first describes the conceptual basis for the procedure. The second offers a computation description and sample problems.
Sprinthall, N. "Personal Development Through Schooling." *Counselor Education and Supervision,* 1975, *14* (4).
  Describes a range of programs that examine issues of human development in classroom settings. Focuses on cognitive competence, moral development, identity, and women's issues.

Tollefson, A. *New Approaches to College Student Development.* New York: Behavioral Publications, 1975.

Somewhat dated. Contains a broad national survey of a wide range of programs in student-development education, including some description of course offerings. Strength lies in the list of programs and contact persons at particular colleges.

Jane Fried is the coordinator of student development, staff training, and research for the Office of Residential Life at the University of Connecticut.

Index

A

Adams, H., 101, 106
Alschuler, A., 22, 25, 106
Anastasi, A., 63
Annotated references, 106-108
Aptitude: redefinition of, 41
Asher, J., 63
Astin, A., 88, 101

B

Barr, M. J., x, 50, 87-102
Bloland, P., 87-101
Bloom, B., 83-85
Boulding, K., 9
Brammer, L., 19, 26
Breen, P., 68, 71
Brown, R., 52, 55
Bundy, R., 9
Buros, O., 64

C

California, University of, at Irvine, 49, 54
Castenanda, C., 19, 26
Chickering, A., 16, 17, 26, 51, 52, 56, 106
Chun, K., 64
Citrin, R., 52, 55
Cobbs, I., 64
Cohen, M., 106
Coley, C., 81, 85
Combs, A., 89, 90, 101
Connecticut, University of, 96
Cousins, N., 7, 9
Cronbach, L. J., 39-41, 47
Crookston, B., x, 14, 18, 26, 55-56, 88, 93, 101, 106

D

Daher, D., ix, 53, 65-72
Darrow, C., 49, 56

Developmental instruction. *See* Student Development education
Dewey, J., 6, 10
Donlon, T., 68, 71
Drum, D. J., 12, 26, 52, 56, 66-67, 72, 106
"Education of the Self," ix, 73-78. *See also* Programs
Erickson, E., 17, 26, 51, 56

F

Faculty consultation, 27-38; model of, 31-38, individual, 33-36, 42-44; group, 36-37
Faculty/student development staff relations: differences between 87-93; how to improve, 97-100
Fairfield, R. P., vii-viii, x, 1-10
Fields, A., 88, 101
French, R., 64
Fried, J., vii-xi, 11-26, 50, 60, 87-102, 103-108
Fund for the Improvement of Postsecondary Education, 31, 39

G

Glass, G. V, 39, 47
Goldman, L., 62, 64
Gronlund, N., 18, 26

H

Hardin, J., 78
Harvard College, 50
Heavilin, R., 95, 101
Heinlein, R., 94, 101
Heslin, R., 107
Higginson, L., 101
Hunt, D. E., 41, 44, 47
Hurst, J., 103, 107

I

Interdisciplinary Studies Program (I-Division), x, 79-85. *See also* Programs
Ivey, A., 22, 25
Ivy, A., 106

J

Johnson, C., ix, 49-56, 104
Johnson, D. W., 19, 26
Jones, J., 107

K

King, P., 88, 101
Klein, E., 49, 56
Knefelkamp, L., vii, xi, 28, 30, 38, 46-47, 103, 107
Knott, G., ix, 53, 65-72
Knott, J. E., 67, 72, 106
Kohlberg, L., 52, 56
Kreps, J., viii, 39-47, 95

L

Leacock, S., 2
Learning contracts, 19-21
Lester, V., ix, 49-56, 104
Levinson, D., 49, 56
Levinson, M., 49, 56
Lippmann, W., 2, 10
Lloyd-Jones, E., 47
Loevinger, J., 52, 56

M

McCreary, J., 12, 26
McKee, B., 49, 56
McLuhan, M., 6, 10
Mager, R., 18, 26
Maslow, A., 17, 26
March, J., 106
Massachusetts, University of, ix, 73
Mentoring, 49-56, 68-69; definition of, 49-51; function of, 51-52; training for, 52-53; programs in, 53-55, 68-69

Miami-Dade Community College, x, 79
Miller, T., 55, 56
Milton, O., 107
Minnesota, University of, viii, 28, 31-32, 37
Morrill, W., 103, 107
Morrison, S. E., 50, 56

N

Northern Illinois, University of, 95

O

Osgood, C., 24, 26

P

Parker, C., vii-viii, xi, 28, 38, 39-47, 95, 103, 107
Perry, W., 17, 21-22, 28-30, 38, 52, 56, 59, 64, 107
Pfeiffer, J., 107
Polak, F., 9-10
Popham, J., 107
Prince, J., 55-56
Prior, J., 87, 101
Programs: examples of, Project Synergy, ix, 53, 65-72, 107; "Education of the Self," ix, 73-78; Interdisciplinary Studies Program (I-Division), x, 79-85; Teaching Improvement Consultation Project (TIC), viii, 31-33
Project Synergy, ix, 53, 65-72. *See also* Programs

R

Rhode Island, University of, ix, 53, 65-66
Rogers C., 16-17, 23-24, 26

S

Sagaria, M., 88, 101
Scarf, M., 49, 56
Schmuck, P., 64
Schmuck, R., 64
Schutz, W., 63-64

Simonton, C., 7, 10
Simonton, S., 7, 10
Simpson, D., viii, 27-38, 42, 95, 103
Sirotnik, K., 107
Smith, M. L., 39, 47
Smith, M. R., 47
Snow, R. E., 39-41, 47
Snygg, D., 89, 101
Sprinthall, N., 107
Student consultation, 44-46
Student Development courses: design of 15-18, 65-67, 73-74, 80-82; identify need for, 15-17; goals of, 17-18; teaching of, 19, 21-24, 67-68, 74-77, 82-83; evaluation of, 24-25, 57-64, 69-71, 78, 83-85; implementation of, 97-100; models of, 97-100; models of, 58-59. See also Programs
Student Development education, 12-13, 104; definition of, vii-viii, 105; constructs of, 12-14; teaching methods in, 14-15, 21-24, 40-47
Student Development educators, 11; skills of, 11, 32; role of, 14-15, 27-28
Student Evaluation of Teaching (SET) 70. See also Student Development courses, evaluation of
Student Teacher Interaction Model (STIM), 20, 22, 24, 60. See also Student Development courses, evaluation of

T

Taylor-Gaunder, T., ix, 57, 64
Teaching-Improvement Consultation Project (TIC), viii, 31-33. See also Programs
Theory of student development, 28-30, 46-47; role of, 52
Tobias, S., 39, 47
Toffler, A., 7, 10
Tollefson, A., 108

W

Watkins, N., x, 13, 26, 79-85
Weinstein, G., ix, 67, 73-78
Weinstein, M., 78
West, J., 1, 10
Widick, C., vii, xi, 28, 30, 38, 46-47, 103, 107
Wilson, W., 2
Whitaker, U., 68, 71
White, E., 101
Whitehead, A., 7, 10-11, 25, 26